From Scenes to Series: Writing Fiction

Mary Ehrenworth and Christine Holley
Lucy Calkins, series editor

Photography by Peter Cunningham

HEINEMANN ◆ PORTSMOUTH, NH

This book is dedicated to Graham, who brings love, light, and laughter to my life. —Christine

This book is dedicated to Rich, who makes life delicious and adventurous. —Mary

Heinemann
361 Hanover Street
Portsmouth, NH 03801–3912
www.heinemann.com

Offices and agents throughout the world

© 2013 by Mary Ehrenworth

The authors and publisher wish to thank those who have generously given permission to reprint borrowed material:

Reprinted with the permission of Simon & Schuster Books for Young Readers, an imprint of Simon & Schuster Children's Publishing Division from *Henry and Mudge and the Happy Cat* by Cynthia Rylant. Copyright © 1990 Cynthia Rylant.

Cataloging-in-Publication data is on file with the Library of Congress.

ISBN-13: 978-0-325-04727-0

Production: Elizabeth Valway, David Stirling, and Abigail Heim
Cover and interior designs: Jenny Jensen Greenleaf
Series includes photographs by Peter Cunningham, Nadine Baldasare, and Elizabeth Dunford
Composition: Publishers' Design and Production Services, Inc.
Manufacturing: Steve Bernier

Printed in the United States of America on acid-free paper
17 16 ML 6

Acknowledgments

THIS BOOK EMERGES out of a long tradition of work with narrative craft at the Teachers College Reading and Writing Project. We are proud to be part of that tradition. Several decades ago, Randy Bomer did breakthrough work with TCRWP teachers on imagining a genre study in fiction. Colleen Cruz and Lucy Calkins's book, *Writing Fiction*, extended that knowledge base. Meanwhile, teachers of primary grades showed us all what is possible with their wonderful work writing Small Moment stories. All of that knowledge base provides shoulders on which this book has been written.

Deciding exactly how best to unfold this unit has been a challenge, and we've written and rewritten the book many times over. In the middle of those rewrites, there have been readers, critics, and counselors who helped us take solid first draft writing and make it clearer and stronger. Notable among these are Amanda Hartman, Rachel Rothman, Julia Mooney, and Kate Montgomery, whose individual and combined wisdom brought joy and insight to this teaching and whose generosity was the greatest gift of all.

Across the books in these units of study, Roberta Lew showed inexhaustible stamina in negotiating with publishers for permission to print texts, even convincing them to reissue out-of-print books. We can't imagine this book without its mentor text—so thank you, Roberta!

Teva Blair, lead editor at Heinemann, has been unflappable, never lowering her incredibly high standards for the clarity of the writing, even in the face of late nights, tight deadlines, and enormous swaths of rough draft text. We have deeply appreciated her talent for untangling our writing knots and her willingness to volunteer for every task.

Thank you, thank you, thank you, especially to the following schools in Manhattan: PS 41 and PS 158; in Brooklyn: PS 154, PS 295, and PS 503; and finally in Queens: PS 182. Several teachers stand out, and we offer them special thanks, in particular, Stefanie Concannon from PS 154 and Marie Mounteer and Priscilla Shen-Ribeiro from PS 295. Thank you (hugely) to Kristi Mraz and Sarah Johnson for your skilled chart making and willingness to roll up your sleeves to help your colleagues.

We also would like to thank our families, who fill our lives with stories that perhaps made their way into the book.

Clearly a big thank you is in order for the staff developers at the Reading and Writing project. The high level of dedication, collaboration, and brilliance is inspirational.

Above all we offer our biggest thanks to Lucy Calkins, who is always a source of inspiration. Thank you for holding the vision for this incredible project and the opportunity to be a part of it. We are grateful for all you do!

The class described in this unit is a composite class, with children and partnerships of children gleaned from classrooms in very different contexts, then put together here. We wrote the units this way to bring you both a wide array of wonderful, quirky, various children and also to illustrate for you the predictable (and unpredictable) situations and responses this unit has created in classrooms across the nation and world.

—Mary and Christine

Contents

Welcome to the Unit

THE URGE TO TELL STORIES begins when children are very young. They love to tell you imagined stories and not entirely real Small Moment stories—and it's amazing to hear the tension and drama they create as storytellers, as they tell the mostly real story of their first try on a bike or the mostly imagined story of why they left the bike out in the rain. Children are dying to "make things up" and to have their stories still sound believable. Allowing children to satisfy this dual urge taps an energy source, and the result is something to behold.

In this final unit in the first-grade curriculum, you'll lead your first-graders into series writing. Yes, series! In the first two bends of the unit, you will lead your children, somewhat step by step, through the process of creating a pretend character, giving that character adventures in more than one booklet, elaborating and revising across books, and finally, creating a "boxed set" of their stories. Along the way, of course, you'll be reminding students to use what they know from their Small Moment writing, and you'll extend those skills. Then, you'll invite students to use all they know to do it again with more independence and agency as they create a second "famous series." On their second go, you'll be steering children to do work at DOK level 4, which is the level of transference and application.

The focus of the unit is on realistic fiction rather than any kind of fiction. We know that some of your students would prefer to write stories about aliens and will even create more pages when they write about aliens. The thing is, while they write more, they rarely write better. When kids truly study what makes a story exciting and still realistic, they end up writing stories that have more heart. Also, kids write best about what they know, and when they realize that their true knowledge of the terrors of riding a bike or lying to a parent after a mishap can find their way into their stories, they inevitably find that they actually have a lot to write about.

This unit will no doubt be a big favorite among your children, so expect that they, and you too, will have lots of fun, but meanwhile this unit also sets children up to do rigorous work that addresses the Common Core State Standards' expectations of them as first-grade writers—and as burgeoning second-grade writers, too. Perhaps most obviously, children will certainly write "narratives in which they recount two or more appropriately sequenced events, include some details regarding what happened, use temporal words to signal event order, and provide some sense of closure" (W.1.3) and "describe actions, thoughts, and feelings" (W.2.3). In fact, they will do much more than that. We fully expect that children will reach toward the second-grade narrative writing standards and sometimes, as they manage event sequences and develop character traits, even toward the third-grade standards. We have designed this unit carefully, so that children begin it, drawing on everything they have learned about narrative writing up until now and simultaneously learning essentials about writing *fictional* narratives. That is, they will draw on their ability to tell what happens first, then next and to bring their characters to life by describing what they do, say, and think.

As the unit progresses, children's understanding of what it means to tell a story with shape and with a satisfying ending will grow. By the second bend, when children begin to write books that go together—that is, series—you will have exceeded the Common Core's expectations of first-graders and will, in fact, also be drawing on the standards in reading. Specifically, children will need to understand how to "describe in depth a character, setting, or event in a story or drama" (R.1.3) to create these in their own stories. They will meanwhile also address reading standards 1.4 and 1.7 as they engage in some reading-writing connections; they'll "identify words and phrases that suggest feelings or appeal to the senses" and will describe a story's characters, setting, or events, using its illustrations and details. In the reading, your children will, in response to your close study of a mentor text, be approximating the second- and third-grade standards 4–6 as they closely study the craft and structure of their touchstone texts.

The work of this unit also sets children up to address many of the speaking and listening, language, and foundational standards. Throughout the unit, children will engage in work with partners, where they'll both speak and listen, and as they write and read, they'll hone their "understanding of the organization and basic features of print" (RF1.1), of "spoken words, syllables and sounds (phonemes)" (RF1.2), and of basic first-grade conventions, including capitalization of names and dates, end punctuation, and conventional spelling of words with common spelling patterns and frequently occurring irregular words.

Throughout this unit, children will work with increasing independence, applying and transferring what they have learned both in prior narrative units and in this unit to lots of realistic fiction books of their own creation. They will be engaging in what Norman Webb describes as level 4 work, that is, working with independence to use what they learn in one context (stand-alone stories) to another (series). As you read this book, you will notice again and again that we challenge children to take stock of what they know, synthesizing skills they have learned across the unit and the first-grade year to push themselves to write more powerfully and with greater precision. Among many other of the first-grade standards in writing, reading, language, and foundations, they will be addressing CCSS W.1.5 as they work, with guidance from teachers and peers, to "add details to strengthen writing as needed."

OVERVIEW OF THE UNIT

Bend I begins with an invitation to children to do something they already love doing—pretending! Because children are natural pretenders, you'll be able to say to them with real—not feigned—confidence, "You're already good at this!" Tell your children that their instinct to pretend, to assume different roles and to see the world through those roles, is a fundamental part of fiction writing. On the first day, you'll teach children that fiction writers call on their pretending skills to invent characters and small moment adventures, and then children will come up with characters of their own, naming them and putting them into imagined scenarios. Throughout the bend, you will encourage your students to write lots of realistic fiction stories quickly and with independence, using all they already know about writing small moments

and bringing stories to life. You'll introduce the notion that characters face a bit of trouble—and that writers then get their characters *out* of trouble to give readers a satisfying ending. You'll engage your children to plan and act out and to bring their lively imaginations to their serious work as writers. Toward the end of the bend, you'll spotlight courageous word choice and spelling and will end by asking your young writers to reflect on their writing, using the narrative checklists to help set new goals.

In the second bend, you'll set your young writers on a new path—to use all they have learned up until now to write series. You'll teach children that series writers put their characters into more than one book, and more than one adventure, and that they give special consideration to what to put into the very first book—Book One—of a series so that readers are set up for the books to follow. As children stay with one or two characters for a few or even half a dozen books, you'll teach them to write with detail and to make their characters talk for different purposes. You'll use *Henry and Mudge* to model as you teach, beginning in this bend and then throughout the duration of this unit. While you won't engage children in a mentor study per say, you and they will lean heavily on an understanding of what beloved series book authors do to make their characters hit home with readers worldwide. The bend ends with a mini-celebration of children's first series. Children will edit their work in preparation for this and create a boxed set (perhaps a cereal box, painted, with a blurb about the famous young author on the back) to showcase their work.

In Bend III, the focus shifts to turning your children into more powerful writers of realistic fiction as you engage students in a study of the genre and of themselves as writers. The bend begins with a mini-inquiry, in which you'll use the class mentor text to determine what writers do to make realistic fiction realistic. You'll teach children that writers call on their own experiences to imagine tiny details they can include in a story to let their readers know a story is realistic. Children will then have a go at this themselves, adding little details to their second series to help readers picture the story in their minds. You'll spotlight how to show, not tell, and will then channel youngsters to think about the structure of their stories as they write chapters with a clear beginning, middle, and end. They'll learn that writers use patterns to elaborate, and they will then draw on all their skills and knowledge as writers of fiction to create even more powerful stories.

In the final bend of the unit, children will prepare to publish their second series. They'll work hard to showcase their work, making it both beautiful and colorful by adding important details to the illustrations, by creating a "meet the author" page to introduce themselves to their readers, and by editing and revising in meaningful ways (with an emphasis on playing with punctuation) to make their work publication-ready. The unit ends with a grand finale, during which an audience will join the class to witness their newly published series.

ASSESSMENT

Before the unit begins, we suggest you take just a bit of time to establish a new baseline understanding of your students' skills as narrative writers so that you know where your children are in this progression at this stage of the year. It will have been several months since children last studied narrative writing, but of course, they will bring with them everything they have learned both this year and last, and you'll want to measure their growth from the start of the year to now.

You may be wondering whether to assess your students by giving them a fiction on-demand task. While teachers have certainly opted to do so, our experience has shown that the writing children produce on-demand when prompted to write a personal narrative is a more accurate reflection of their capacity for narrative writing than is the fictional writing they produce under the same circumstances. Think of it this way: how apt would you be to showcase your understanding of narrative writing if you had to first come up with a fictional character and fictional circumstances, including trouble the character faces, all on the spot? And even if you somehow came up with ideas for these components, how likely would you be to do your best small moment writing? Wouldn't you give greater attention to writing well if instead of having to weave a tale out of thin air, you could instead just tell a story about your own life—one that you knew inside and out? Consider this, too: the exact same basic qualities of writing that make a strong personal narrative make a strong piece of fiction: elements such as showing, not telling, writing with detail, writing with voice, including a blend of dialogue and action, placing the reader into the setting, and so forth.

Some of you may question whether an on-demand assessment is even necessary. After all, this is the children's first time writing fiction, you may argue. There's a reason we believe this assessment is crucial: the short amount of time it takes to set children up to complete this task is nothing compared to the invaluable, endless data it provides. Not only will it serve as a measure for children's growth across the unit, but it will also help to track their growth

across the year. You'll be able to see improvements each child has made—and to share this with the kids, themselves, and their parents. If you write narrative report cards or have another meeting with parents planned, you can say, "This is what your child's writing was like at the very start of the year, and this is what it was like at the start of this unit. And look, this is what he (or she) can do at the end of the unit!"

In *Writing Pathways: Peformance Assessments and Learning Progressions, K–5,* we'll provide you with instruments—including checklists and learning progressions—that will help you to see where, in the trajectory of writing development, each of your students lies.

For this initial assessment to provide accurate baseline data on your writers' narrative skills, be careful not to scaffold your students' work during this assessment. After all, the worse they do, the more dramatic their progress will be! You'll want to simply remind students of the basic qualities you expect in a piece of narrative writing, then step back and leave them to their own devices. We recommend you give students the following prompt to start them off.

> "I'm really eager to understand what you can do as writers of narratives, of stories, so today, will you please write the best personal narrative, the best Small Moment story, that you can write? Make this be the story of one time in your life. You might focus on just a scene or two. You'll only have forty-five minutes to write this true story, so you'll need to plan, draft, revise, and edit in one sitting. Write in a way that allows you to show off all you know about narrative writing."

Because assessments are more valid across grades if the testing conditions are the same, we also recommend you give students additional specifications that we know most first-graders will ignore (but some will find helpful.) You can find these in *Writing Pathways: Performance Assessments and Learning Progressions, K–5.*

It is, of course, your school's decision whether it is acceptable to alter this protocol. We simply want to remind you that if you do so, it is important that you are transparent about this and that you and your grade level colleagues agree on the same alterations because it's essential that children across classrooms do the assessment under identical conditions. This way, you can accurately compare data across the grade, which will be invaluable to growing your own understanding and performance as first-grade teachers.

Because your children will be familiar with the format of on-demand assessments by this stage in the year, they won't need much to get started. We suggest that when you tell students the prompt and show them the chart of suggestions, kids be already at their regular writing seats, with familiar paper to draw on and a supply of additional pages if they want them.

Once children have completed the assessment, we suggest you duplicate their work so that each child has a copy of what he or she has written. By having the on-demand writing close on hand, writers will have a comparison piece against which to measure the subsequent writing they do across the unit. Periodically across the unit, then, you'll remind them to look between the stories they are writing now and the one they wrote at the start of the unit, to check that they are growing as narrative writers.

You, meanwhile, will assess where each writer falls in the Narrative Writing Learning Progression and where the bulk of your class falls, letting that information inform the upcoming unit of study. Read each student's draft, comparing it to the exemplar texts, and then read the descriptors to determine the precise ways each student can improve. Many of your children will probably be working toward achieving end-of-second-grade standards, which is very exciting. No text will match the checklist in its entirety, so don't be knocked off kilter if a piece of writing has a few descriptors that show a great deal of Needs Improvement. The descriptors will be particularly useful as you share with children concrete steps they can take to make their writing better. That is, if a writer's narrative is level 1, you and that writer can look at the descriptors of, say, character development for level 2 and note whether the writing adheres to those. If so, tell that child (or your whole class if this is broadly applicable), "You used to develop the people in your stories by . . . ," and read the descriptors from the prior level, "but now you are . . . ," and read the level 2 descriptor. "Can I give you a pointer about a way to make your writing even better? You can . . . ," and read from the level 3 descriptor. You can even say, "Let me show you an example," and then cite a section of the level 2 and the level 3 exemplar texts.

GETTING READY

Probably the most important work to do in readiness for this unit is reading work. You'll want to read aloud some delightful and enticing realistic fiction stories to immerse the children in the genre they will be writing. Choose stories you love, stories that are part of series—since the children will write series—and stories that are within their range as writers and readers in terms of length and complexity. In this unit of study, we pay special attention to the Henry and Mudge series by Cynthia Rylant. We look very closely at *Henry and Mudge and the Happy Cat* as well as the first book in the series.

In addition, we suggest you get ready by . . . writing stories! The unit is going to make so much more sense to you and you'll feel so much more prepared if you've done the writing and faced the challenges that your children will face. So prepare your own collection of stories about one character that you can use as your demonstrate writing in front of the children. It's often great fun to do this work with colleagues. Work on these stories together, each writing some texts that you can use for the predictable small groups and one-on-one conferences you'll have, as well for minilessons. Find an afternoon, a sunny table, and some friends, and compose some rollicking fiction stories. We tend to keep in mind the range of interests and personalities in our classes, so while we might have written stories that were more internal, emotional struggles because that's what we tend to think of, we make sure to think of Ralph Fletcher's advice from *Boy Writers*, and we also push ourselves toward action, moments of grossness, and the kinds of characters and events that will reach various children in our class.

Of course, be sure your writing center is stocked with paper with various numbers of lines and a picture box and maybe even paper full of lines and no picture box for those who are ready. Keep the revision strips and revision pens available too.

Lastly, we suggest that you start to collect cereal boxes since as a celebration we ask kids to create a boxed set of their collection of stories. Each student will need two cereal boxes, and you'll need a couple to experiment with. You may want to go around the school as well, or raid you own shelves, for some beloved box sets, whether it's Captain Underpants or Misty of Chincoteague. Just handling these sets, and writing in their shadow, will inspire all of you.

Serious Fiction Writers Do Some Serious Pretending

IN THIS SESSION, you'll teach children that writers call on their pretending skills to invent characters and Small Moment adventures.

GETTING READY

✔ A fiction story you have written to use as a demonstration text, one with a character and a Small Moment story (see Teaching)

✔ Partners sitting next to each other

✔ Five-page booklets on hand in the meeting area for student use during rehearsal, if desired

✔ "How to Write a Realistic Fiction Book" chart, prewritten on chart paper, to introduce during the active engagement

✔ Writing center stocked with lots of five-page booklets and a basket of individual sheets in case kids need to add on, including the revision strips they used in the personal narrative unit. Writing paper can have space for a picture and five to six lines for writing words. One basket might have paper with only lines.

✔ A few books from a series. We highlight Henry and Mudge and use *Henry and Mudge and the Happy Cat* as a mentor text later in this unit.

COMMON CORE STATE STANDARDS: W.1.3, W.1.8, RL.1.1, RL.1.3, RL.1.10, RL.2.3, SL.1.1, SL.1.4, L.1.1, L.1.2

FICTION IS A PERFECT GENRE FOR YOUNG CHILDREN because, almost anytime you observe children during playtime, what you will see is that they are already walking in the shoes of characters, dreaming up all sorts of scenarios, and playacting their way toward solutions. Hang out in the block area or listen to kids at the sandbox or join a group in the far corner of the playground, and you'll find yourself eavesdropping as children serve soup at a restaurant, quiet a fussing baby, board a train, man the controls on a speedboat, or tame a growling dog.

You may launch this unit by conveying to children, "You're already good at this!" You'll have accomplished something very important if you let your children know that their instinct to pretend, to assume different roles and to see the world through those roles, is a fundamental part of fiction writing.

Almost all children grow up pretending. Ironically, studies such as *The Last Child in the Woods* by Richard Louv (2008), suggest that children in more highly scheduled and highly protective environments are sometimes left to themselves less and pretend less than those who experience what has been named "benevolent neglect," the kids who are left alone to play in the back woods, down by the pond, or in the overgrown lot next to their building. This finding suggests that your classroom may contain a few children who haven't pretended as fully as others. These children will need this unit more than all your others. They need it not only to write fiction, but also to read fiction, for the thin line is not just between drama and writing. It is also between believing in drama and reading—what it is to lose oneself in a story, to fall through the rabbit hole, to allow oneself to be transported to a world of talking lions and satyrs.

You'll see this unit begins, then, by inviting children to bring their love of pretend play into the writing workshop. You're tapping into their instinct to dress up, to become someone else, and saying, "This is how people come up with a fiction story, so go to it." In today's session, you don't load kids up with ten strategies for generating stories or with cautionary advice about how to avoid the worst traps when writing fiction. Your emphasis is not on caution signs at all. Instead, the message is "Welcome. Come in. Get Started!"

Here's what to expect as you get started: In the first session of the unit, children will have an opportunity to remember what they know about small moments, and will generate and write a story. Some children may finish one story and start a second. A few may write a story that is long enough for them to write across more than one day. You can expect that your writers won't write perfectly in sync, starting a new story each day and finishing it magically as workshop nears the time for share. Instead, they'll lean on their imaginations, which are chock-full of ideas for pretending, to start new stories when one is completed. In Bend II, you'll have the chance to introduce the idea of writing series. A series can be a dozen books or as few as three. Again, don't expect synchronicity! Some children will write one short series and start another. Others may create a little cast of characters, and a sequence of problems that ensue in multiple books of a long series. In this bend you'll see a focus on getting children to write a lot and on helping them develop some agency so they harness their own powers before they take on the challenge of creating a series in Bend II.

"You're tapping into children's instinct to dress up, to become someone else, and saying, 'This is how people come up with a fiction story, so go to it.'"

Serious Fiction Authors Do Some Serious Pretending

CONNECTION

Offer up an analogy between make-believe and fiction writing, between pretend play and fiction characters, to generate enthusiasm and set the stage for the unit.

"Writers, I think you know that we will be writing realistic fiction books, because we've been reading some stories and talking about this for days! Realistic fiction stories seem like they're real. They could really happen. But you still get to make them up. Realistic fiction books tell stories about stuff that could happen but that you've pretended. You pretend all the time. I know that when you play, you've pretended about boys who find lost dogs, and girls who stand up to bullies, and you've pretended all sorts of other stories, too.

"Well, guess what? We are about to get serious about pretending in our writing!"

◆ **Name the teaching point.**

"Today I want to teach you that when you write realistic fiction, you *imagine* a pretend character. Then you pretend things about that character—where the character is, what the character does, and *especially* the trouble he or she gets in. Fiction writers give the character real-life adventures."

TEACHING

Demonstrate by creating a pretend character and coming up with a Small Moment adventure for that character.

"So it's all a game of pretend, which you are *seriously* good at.

"Now I'll show you how I pretend about a character and imagine stuff about her that I could put in a story. You will see that I think up some trouble for this pretend character, then write one of these adventures as a realistic fiction book. Watch, and as I do this, you can get started imagining your character. You mostly want to think about the trouble your character might get into. Give a quiet thumbs up when you start to have an idea for your pretend character.

In any unit of study, your first minilesson conveys the big picture of the unit and is a welcoming invitation into the heart of the work. When you write your own units of study, take note of the way session one in all of these units goes straight to the heart of writing. This is not a time for your teaching to feel swamped with procedural detail.

We don't just explain the process of generating a story idea. Instead, this process is enacted. We reenact the process for children as a kind of mini-drama, starting with the words "Watch me." Reenacting (or dramatizing) gives children a demonstration. Demonstrations are vastly more effective than explanations.

GRADE 1: FROM SCENES TO SERIES

"Each of you will do this differently, but for me, I'm first going to imagine a name and a place. You can do the same thing if it helps you get started."

I closed my eyes for a moment, as if thinking. "Hmm. I've always *wished* my name was Gretchen, because that sounds to me like a little girl who lives near the woods. And I've always *wished* I had a tree fort in the forest. So my character is going to be Gretchen, who has a tree fort. I know something about tree forts, so I can pretend well about a tree fort, and make it very real," I said, signaling with a thumbs up to remind children I'd asked for them to let me know when they started to have a story idea. "I bet some of you are starting to think of characters too."

I opened my eyes and noted that some kids had their thumbs up. I nodded at them, smiled at the others encouragingly, and went on. "Now I have to think of some trouble that Gretchen might get into."

I demonstrated telling possible trouble to come up with some ideas for stories. "Hmm . . . well, Gretchen was often playing in her tree fort, and there's a lot of trouble that could happen near a fort." I closed my eyes for a moment as if imagining. "I'm picturing the fort, with a girl in it . . . maybe Gretchen got in trouble by falling out of the tree fort . . . or she got stuck up there . . . or, let's see . . . she forgot the time . . . or I know, maybe Gretchen found a hurt animal there! That certainly is some trouble that Gretchen could run into."

I opened my eyes. "Yes, I think I'll tell the story of the time when Gretchen found a hurt animal by the fort—and if I finish that book, I can always tell another of these 'Gretchen in the fort' stories!

"So . . . let me try out what might happen across my fingers, like you've done so many times."

I began imagining the scene: "So . . . I'm picturing the scene . . . Gretchen found some kind of animal who is hurt near her fort. Now let me rehearse it." Then I began to tell the story across my fingers, opening a finger in my hand for each part. "First, Gretchen heard the sound of an animal . . . and she came closer. Next, she realized it was a bird and she was afraid it might peck her. Then, she decided to be brave . . . finally, she scooped the bird in her sweater and went to look for help at home!"

Debrief in a way that is transferable to another day, another workshop.

"You're imagining your character?" A few more thumbs began to go up. I nodded. "So, what did I do to think up a story? I imagined a character. I gave that character a name and a place. Then I thought about trouble the character could get into. Here's a tip, writers! I didn't try to put every trouble I could think of into one story! I zoomed in on one trouble, just like we learned how to do in Small Moments. Then I tried rehearsing a story about one time when my character gets into trouble, across my fingers. No big deal, because we're so good at pretending!"

Notice the invitational language: "You can do the same." In Choice Words *(2004), Peter Johnston has shown that the language of invitation better supports independence.*

By demonstrating that a writer zooms in on one moment, you reinforce the "smallness" of small moments. You also reinforce that writers can return to ideas for stories at any time, to write more than one story. It's helpful for young writers to know that coming up with ideas is no big deal, that they can go onto a new piece right away.

If you hold up your fingers as you proceed bit by bit through your story, this will remind students they can match each part of their story to one finger as well, as they learned in previous units. Keep in mind that whether children tell their story across their fingers or by touching each page of a blank booklet as they say what they might write, the big lesson is that writers rehearse for writing. It doesn't matter which strategy writers choose to do this work.

ACTIVE ENGAGEMENT

Invite partners to plan as you've just done, imagining a pretend character with a name, place, and real-life trouble he or she can get into.

"I bet you're dying to try this. There are little tricks that can help with pretending. One is to come up with a name that you like. How about if, right now, you each think about what name you will give your character? For a second, let's be quiet so you can think about that and decide."

As I watched children settle on a name, I coached quietly, channeling their thinking through a sequence of further thoughts. "Then think where this character will be. If you have a bunch of possible places, that's okay. Just choose one for now. It's great if it's a place you know a lot about." I gave children a second of silence.

"Now, what real-life trouble do you think your character might get into?" I waited another few seconds. "Which trouble do you want to write a story about? For a second, let's just be quiet and plan."

Remind children that they know how to rehearse by telling their story to their partner.

After a minute, I said, "Writers, earlier this year you wrote stories. Remember to do all that you already learned to do! For example, earlier, you learned that when writing a Small Moment story, it helps to touch and tell across the pages of your booklet or across your fingers. Take a moment to rehearse your story with your partner. Partner 1, you go first. I'll be watching as you use your fingers or the pages of a booklet to help you tell one thing your character will do and then the next thing. Go ahead, turn and story-tell."

I listened in, coaching to help students generate realistic characters and plot ideas. As I listened in, I said things like, "Whoa, zoom in on one small moment! Which of those stories will you tell?" Or, "Wait, wait, where is he at the start of the story?" Or "Let's keep it real! Maybe he meets a scary bully rather than a zombie!"

Invite the second partner to give it a go. If many children need the reminder to focus on a small moment, take this opportunity to give the children feedback to focus on small moments. Recall a familiar metaphor, perhaps saying writers write not watermelon stories but seed stories.

"Writers, let's give Partner 2 a chance. I'm going to give you one super important tip as you go forward. Remember what you know about focusing on a small moment. Think seed, not watermelon! Writers, you need to zoom in on just one small moment. Try that now, okay? Like, for me, it's going to be the one time when Gretchen found the bird and decided to rescue it. Give it a try, Partner 2! Show us how to tell a seed story that is one time, one trouble." I used my finger to emphasize one trouble, and as I said seed I showed a very small space between finger and thumb.

"Writers, I bet you can't wait to get started writing your realistic fiction books. And I can't wait to read them! I've created a new chart for this new kind of writing you will be doing this unit. Even though you will be writing realistic fiction books, you can get started almost the same way you got started writing your Small Moment stories and your teaching books. First, you think of a pretend character, plan, then write!" (See Figure 1–1.)

Notice that although the entire minilesson supports the teaching point, this doesn't mean that there is no new information in the teaching or active engagement sections of a minilesson. Instead, there are not only a demonstration and a time for supported practice, but also lots of little tips are woven throughout.

You may want to decide how tightly you are holding all your students right away to realistic fiction. Undoubtedly some of your writers will prefer to write about monsters. On the other hand, Ralph Fletcher in Boy Writers (2006) shows how you can lure these same action-driven writers into realistic fiction by allowing farts and vomit and all sorts of hilarious and yucky stuff. We're going that route, because experience has shown that especially with the help of a good mentor text, realistic fiction tends to lead to writing with more meaning.

As your writers rehearse their stories, do your best to listen in. This is a time to be especially alert to danger signs that writers aren't really telling a story yet. If some writers are listing ideas, or others are telling "every time" stories, you'll either help them quickly zoom in, or plan to pull those writers into a small group to give support around writing Small Moment stories.

> How to Write a Realistic Fiction Book
>
> 1. Think of a pretend character
>   - Give the character a name
>   - Imagine a place
>   - Imagine the trouble your character gets into
> 2. Plan
>   - Touch and tell, sketch across pages
> 3. Write!

LINK

Send the children off to write, tucking in what you're expecting to see as you send them off.

"Let's get started writing! I can't wait to see the characters you create and the trouble they get into! I can tell you're going to be writing a lot of sentences, on many pages!"

FIG. 1–1 "How to Write a Realistic Fiction Book" charts

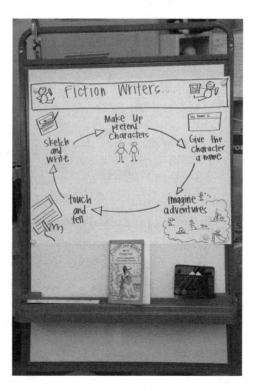

With Help, All Your Children Can Write Up a Storm!

TODAY YOU MAY NOTICE that some kids jump at the idea of making up a character and immediately begin writing a book. As you scan the classroom you may also see some kids not getting started so easily. If you notice more than one child who seems stumped, you may decide to hold a small group focused on generating ideas for fiction writing.

You might begin your small group by reminding the children of the big things you did in the minilesson: you picked a name for your character, then thought of a place the character might be, and some trouble the character might get into. Then you could coach children to do the same, watching for where they get stuck. To get started, ask each child the name of his or her character. This will get them going faster than you might think. As your children each announce the name, you can say, "Okay, great. What trouble will Joe get into? What will happen to Philip in your story?" Your demonstration might go something like this:

"So where will *you* (your character) be at the start of your story? I think my character, Gretchen, will be right in front of this." I balled up a piece of paper and put it on the floor. "That's the animal!" I acted as if I heard a sound and said out of the side of my mouth, "peep, peep, CAW! Peep, peep, CAW!" Then I crouched onto my hands and knees, and approached the paper slowly. I paused after acting, and dictated the following, jotting it down quickly on a piece of chart paper.

> Gretchen heard a noise. "Peep, peep, CAW! Peep, peep, CAW!"
> "What is that?" she thought. She crouched down on the path . . .

"See how I acted out the start of the story, and then I wrote it down quickly? You can do this too. Why don't you act out to the person next to you what your character will be doing at the first line of your book. See if they can help you imagine the details so you can capture the start of your story." Once the children had done this, I sent them off to keep writing.

If you see kids really having trouble, you may simply bring them back to what they did when writing small moments. In Small Moment stories children thought about something they did or something that happened to them. So you can say that in realistic fiction writing, a writer can do the same thing, but instead of writing what happened

MID-WORKSHOP TEACHING   Getting Started All By Yourself!

"Writers, can I stop you? I was just working with Annabel. Annabel did something really surprising. She finished one book. Then, I saw her put down her book, close her eyes for a moment, wave her fingers around, and then pick up another booklet! Here's what I said to her, writers."

I leaned in, pointing a finger at Annabel, who smirked. "Annabel," I said. "Are you already starting a second story? Don't you need to think quietly of an idea, and rehearse it with your partner? Don't you need more time to think? Aren't you getting AHEAD of yourself, Annabel?" I said this last sentence with much drama, as if rebuking Annabel.

I looked around at the children. "Well, writers, Annabel explained that she *had* thought quickly and she *had* told her story to herself across her fingers. She had already done that important work, all by herself! And now she was starting her second book, all by herself!"

"If that works for you, writers, if you finish one story and feel like you can tell a second one to yourself, imagining the character and the trouble he or she will get into, and telling the small moment adventure across your fingers so you're ready to write—go to it! Annabel, you're inspiring writers to be even more powerful, all by themselves!"

to him- or herself, the writer pretends it happened to a character. In other words, if you fell off your bike, maybe today you'll write a story about a pretend character named Graham who fell off his bike.

As you confer one-on-one, you may coach kids to story-tell versus summarize. You will most likely be coaching kids to story-tell across pages of a blank booklet like they learned to do for small moments. You might refer to the "How to Write a Realistic Fiction Book" chart you introduced today as well. This will help get them started so they can move to sketching and writing quickly on Day One. Remember that since it is Day One, a big priority is to build excitement and create a buzz about the fabulous fiction writers they will become during the next few weeks, reminding children how much fun it is to pretend and to write up a storm.

FIG. 1–2 The demonstration piece can raise the level of your children's writing by explicitly modeling the narrative craft you hope they'll use—such as action and dialogue. Often children will intuitively emulate your technique, especially if the demo text is clear and simple.

To Be Continued
Stopping and Starting as a Fiction Writer

Offer tips for how authors get ready to dive back in when they come back to their writing the next day.

I called the children back to the meeting area with their materials. Once they were gathered, I said, "Fiction writers, experienced authors often give advice to up-and-coming writers. And one tip that a lot of authors give, is this: as you wrap up one day of writing, it's good to use your last few minutes to begin a next page, or sentence, or book—something that is 'to be continued.' That way, when you sit down to write tomorrow, you can jump right in and continue your work. The hardest thing for a writer is starting with an empty page."

I held up Joshua's books. "Look what Joshua has done, children." I opened up his first book, to the page that read, THE END. Then I opened the beginning of his second book, which already had a sketch on the first page, and one sentence. "Joshua finished his book. He did that just a few minutes ago, and it would have been easy for him to sit back, relax, and say, 'I'm done!' But instead, he wanted to be powerful so he started a sketch for his next story. And then, he even started *his first sentence*, which means tomorrow, he can dive right in as a writer. No sitting around saying, 'I don't know what to write about!'"

I looked around at the children. "This is a big deal for writers. Getting something started for your next writing day, making that 'to be continued' feeling a ritual, can make you a much more powerful writer. Right now, can you look at where you're wrapping up today? Go ahead, open your booklets, find where you are finishing—and put your finger on that page." I waited for children to find their place. "Now, while your ideas are fresh, will you make a note on the *next* page, which will help you get started tomorrow, fast and furious? Maybe it's the first sentence of the next part of your story. Maybe it's the sketch that will start your next book. Go ahead, do just enough that you'll be able to jump in. Then let's put your 'to be continued' work in your folders. Tomorrow you can jump back in easily, right into writing."

Session 2

Writers Develop a "Can-Do," Independent Attitude

I N *CHOICE WORDS* (2004), Peter Johnston creates an image of children as active agents, able to take responsibility for their own learning and the well-being of their learning community. Johnston describes the language that accomplished teachers use to encourage this kind of agency and caring. It is the language of "I like the way you figured that out," and "What are your thoughts on that?" rather than "Please do what I tell you . . . now!" Before we read *Choice Words*, when a child said, "I need a pencil," we often quickly put one in his hand—anything to get him back to writing—whereas now we hear Peter whispering in our ear, and we respond, "Do you need help with that problem or do you think you can solve it yourself?" Peter's influence has meant that we're more willing to take the time to cultivate agency and problem solving as important skills.

When you read Peter's book, or if you are ever able to hear him speak and see some of his classroom videos, you'll probably find yourself entranced at how children in his studies have learned agency and problem solving. What you quickly come to realize is that the "can-do" attitude of even the youngest students (many of those whom Peter studies are in kindergarten and first grade) has been cultivated by the teachers. These teachers work hard at waiting, at prompting, at giving very small cues so that children can work to solve their own problems. It takes a lot of patience to teach this way. It's not just a free-for-all, though. What Peter shows is how to take advantage of the natural messiness of classrooms so that the smallest moment (such as a child not having a pencil) can be a significant learning event.

You can also anticipate some of these problem-solving/take charge moments, which is what this session is about. In the last session, children began realistic fiction stories. Some of them may be deep in one story, some may have started a second. Some have imagined more than one story about the same character, and others will have created stories about different characters. All of that was left deliberately open, as the main intent was to get children pretending, and writing, a lot right away. Now they could benefit from some writing time before being introduced to another strategy, so that they can get lots of pages written with their initial story ideas. It's also important for your writers to realize that they

IN THIS SESSION, you'll teach children that writers develop a "can-do" attitude and give themselves orders, using all the tools at hand to work independently and keep going.

GETTING READY

✔ Your own metaphor or story that exemplifies being independent (see Connection)

✔ "How to Write a Realistic Fiction Book" chart from Session 1 (see Connection)

✔ A list of strategies that you hope your students will remember to do to be independent writers. You can refer to the list in the minilesson (see Active Engagement).

✔ A student's writing folder that will serve as a good model for the class. Choose a folder that has a large quantity of writing in it. You will use this in the mid-workshop teaching to show kids that their writing folders are a resource they can use to become more expert, independent writers.

COMMON CORE STATE STANDARDS: W.1.3, W.1.5, W.1.8, W.2.3, RL.1.1, RL.1.3, RL.2.3, SL.1.1, L.1.1, L.1.2

can keep going without a new strategy every time. You can help children realize that they know a lot about how to help themselves. In this case, how to start a new story and to keep going as fiction writers. These units of study are full of sessions such as these, which give you an opportunity to assess your children's independent prowess and stamina. Watch for what they remember and apply, not only from yesterday, but from earlier units of study—strategies for choosing paper wisely, for working with a partner, for getting themselves "unstuck," for getting a lot of writing done, as well as for what they know about small moments and narrative writing. There's a lot to be learned from watching your writers set their own expectations, and for how they respond to your expectations.

"You can help children realize that they know a lot about how to help themselves. In this case, how to start a new story and to keep going as writers."

Writers Develop a "Can-Do," Independent Attitude

CONNECTION

Create a picture of what it means to have a can-do, independent attitude.

"Writers, yesterday after school I was at the playground, and I watched a kid named Sam. Sam has been learning to ride a bike. Usually, his babysitter has Sam sit on the bench while she is helping his baby sister out of the stroller. Then she helps him get started. She tells him what to do. She says, 'Put on your helmet, Sam!' And Sam puts on his helmet. She says, 'Pedal faster, Sam!' Sam pedals faster.

"But today was different. Today while Sam's babysitter was unstrapping his baby sister from the stroller, I saw Sam getting out his helmet on his own. I saw him get his helmet out and begin to whisper. He was whispering to himself. 'Put on your helmet, Sam!' Then he got on his bike and he whispered to himself, 'Pedal faster, Sam!' And he pedaled faster.

"Sam reminded me of you. He remembered everything he needed to do to ride that bike. And you can remember everything you need to do to write realistic fiction books.

"We did a lot of new things yesterday, and some things you already knew. I taught you to . . . " I pointed to the chart as I read aloud.

How to Write a Realistic Fiction Book

1. Think of a pretend character
   - Give the character a name
   - Imagine a place
   - Imagine the trouble your character gets into
2. Plan
   - Touch and tell, sketch across pages
3. Write!

◆ COACHING

One of the ways you can help children assume the role of being their own teacher and coach is for you to let them in on your goals for your teaching. This simple episode gives you a way to explicitly teach children that the goal is for them to internalize all the teaching they have received and to be able to draw on that teaching without needing constant input from you.

Your anchor chart will be a scaffold for the children and you, to help them work with more independence. "Remember, you can start a story by using these strategies . . . " you'll say, pointing to this familiar record of your teaching.

Name the teaching point.

"Today I want to teach you that writers take charge of their own writing and give themselves orders. They think about the work they need to do next and almost whisper little assignments to themselves, such as, 'Now I need to . . .' and 'Next I should. . . .'"

TEACHING

Act out the part of being a self-sufficient writer working on a second story. Pretend to resist the temptation to be independent.

"Writers, I really want to give this a try. I'll act out the part of a first-grade writer. If I get stuck, can you help me out? Don't yell things out, though. Whisper them so I can pretend I thought of it! Let's see. Yesterday when we finished, like you, I did one thing to help me get started on a new story. But I didn't do enough! I wrote . . . 'Gretchen climbed her tree fort again.' But I didn't make a sketch, and now I can't remember what I wanted to write about—what trouble Gretchen would get in. So I need an idea."

I looked around abjectly. "Hmm, I should . . . ask my friend for an idea. No, that's not taking charge. Ask my teacher for help. No, that's not taking charge . . . copy someone near me. No, that's not it. Hide in the bathroom? No."

I closed my eyes as if desperately remembering. "Help me out here. I can . . . " From all corners of the room, kids began to whisper instructions. I pretended not to hear for a moment, eyes closed, face scrunched up, muttering under my breath, "What do I already know about writing fiction stories?"

Rally children to help you take charge of your writing.

Children continued whispering instructions. "Make her do something." "Think of some trouble." "Pretend to be your character." As more instructions and orders came from the children, I took in what they were whispering, and whispered it to myself. "Pretend to be the charachter! Right, I should imagine her climbing up the fort " And then, "Give the character some trouble. Right! Maybe Gretchen could slip or maybe her brother is blocking the entrance. Phew! I'm getting started now."

Debrief in ways that cull overarching principles that can guide writers in the future.

"Writers, did you see how I worked at remembering how fiction writers get started? Then I whispered some directions, or orders, to myself. It's like I was thinking, 'I'm in charge! So get started!' You were helping me, so you'll be even better at this than I was."

As you teach, have your back to the chart so the children can see it, but you can't.

Over and over in this series, you will notice that when we want to highlight a feature or characteristic one of the ways we do so is to show its opposite. We define or dramatize about what something is by contrasting it with what it's not. Here we demonstrate self-sufficiency by showing that we are tempted to be needy writers, but resist that temptation.

ACTIVE ENGAGEMENT

Recruit writers to try getting themselves started, writing another fiction book.

"Give this a try for a moment. Some of you are starting another book—others of you are deep into a second or third. You may already have started a sentence or a sketch—what comes next? Not what would you write next—what would you do next? Think for a moment of a couple orders you might whisper to yourself that will help you keep going independently. Then whisper them so your partner can hear as well."

The children thought, then whispered. I repeated some of what they were saying, adding in some ideas to stir up the pot, as if some children had said them. "Oh yes, I'm hearing you say that you will get paper with lots of lines. I love that! That is independent. Some of you are saying you can set a goal to finish this book in one day. Some of you realized that you have to get your character in a place and facing some trouble. Great!"

Summarizing what children say enables you to add in what they are "sort of" saying, so that you raise the discourse level. It's also more efficient than interrupting the flow of the lesson to call on students.

Record some ideas about what it might look like to write with more expertise, independence, and daring. Include suggestions that stir up your writers to big work and big *attitudes*.

After a bit, I convened them, consolidating what they had said, occasionally crediting a child who authored an idea. "Writers, that was amazing! I heard whispered orders to 'get a booklet and get started!' Pete said, 'Choose some paper with more lines!' I heard, 'Imagine another character, and some trouble for that character. And I heard, 'Give your character an adventure they won't forget!' I even heard, 'Make sure your reader can read it!' Great orders."

LINK

Send children off to write with a concise reminder of the teaching they can draw upon.

"Okay, writers, time for you to show off now. I'm going to admire you as you give yourself directions. When you feel like you need some help, first think about what you know, and try whispering to yourself. Giving yourself orders often keeps your engine going as a writer."

"I'm going to admire you as you..." is one of your most powerful teaching phrases. Help your children envision what you're hoping they'll do—with invitational language.

Acting as Audience and Journalist

Observing Children as They Write and Reinforcing Positive Behaviors

I SUSPECT YOU WILL SEE CHILDREN EAGER TO SHOW OFF how independent they can be. On this day, immediately after the minilesson, you will want to walk around the room oohing and ahhing as you acknowledge all the risk taking going on. Offer simple words and signals of encouragement, like a thumbs up. You may see some kids only gesturing toward something in a small way, and a simple recognition can reinforce for kids to work with zeal. Reinforcing positive behaviors is a very effective strategy to get things up and running quickly.

You are basically acting as if the children already know how to write realistic fiction books, even though it is only Day Two. For example, you may sit at a table and announce something you see one student doing that you hope they all will begin doing. You may say, "Piper, those detailed sketches are really going to help you write lots of words. And Etta, your character's big adventure happens at the beach. You can make the sound and feel of the beach a big part of your story." Or "Amos, you are really becoming such a grown-up writer. You didn't wait to go back and finish yesterday's story before starting a new one. You are really using your time wisely." Naming positive behaviors that you see writers doing is a reminder of the work that all students can do.

You can also act like an interested audience, someone who can't help but make comments on the work kids have done, such as "Oh Annabel, I can't wait to find out what happens to your character, Mary, at the aquarium. I'm so worried she got lost from her class. I hope she will be okay!" This keeps ideas floating around for those who are stuck. As you move around writers, building enthusiasm, you will want to be on the lookout for writers who need more focused support.

You may find that some of your students are like Mohammad, who seemed to be satisfied with only two sentences of writing on a page. You will want to push writers who aren't producing much text to add more, to elaborate. It might sound something like "Mohammad, I can see you did so many of the things that fiction writers do. You drew pictures and then wrote the words across pages of a book. *And* you even made up a

MID-WORKSHOP TEACHING
Using Writing Folders to Be More Expert and Independent

"Writers, can I have your eyes on me for a moment?" I stood near Justin's desk. I had prepped Justin for what we would say and do next. We played it out dramatically, very campy. "Ready? Can you see and hear? Okay." I lowered my voice like a newscaster in an ancient tomb. "We're here with Justin. Justin has just found a secret storage place full of examples that will help him be a more expert writer. This is an exciting moment for all of us. Justin, can you share this secret storage place with us?" Justin nodded slowly. "Thank you, Justin. That is very generous of you. Justin, lead us to the secret storage place." Justin looked around the room slowly. I followed his gaze, pointing at charts, then dictionaries, then bookshelves. Justin shook his head. Slowly, he raised his writing folder over his head, then held it straight above, as if it were precious and heavy.

I gasped. "This is it, writers! In a never-before-seen moment, Justin shares with us the secret storage place, where writers can find examples of what expert writers do. It is . . . *your writing folders*. Who would have guessed, that hidden within these folders are some of our past charts and tools to show you how to unfreeze people, to use your word-solving powers, and much more! Thank you, Justin, for sharing this *amazing* discovery with us. Remember, take some of these tools out to help you as you are writing and rereading and checking your work."

I looked around the room, nodding as if amazed. Already, kids were reaching for their folders too, giggling.

character and wrote a small moment about him. You knew to do all those things so easily! I'm wondering if you'd be game for another challenge?"

Because Mohammad was eager for me to up the ante, I said, "Do you remember that once writers have finished a book—or even part of a book—they shift from being a writer to being a reader? One way to read your own writing is to think 'What else would I want to know? Could I elaborate? What have I done before that I can do now?'"

Mohammad read his fiction book (see Figure 2–1), pointing to places where he said, "I can add more to this part."

For example, Mohammad pointed to page 2. "I could add something here, maybe." I nodded, waiting for him to tell me what he could add, but he simply waited also. I nudged him to say what he could add, but he only shrugged.

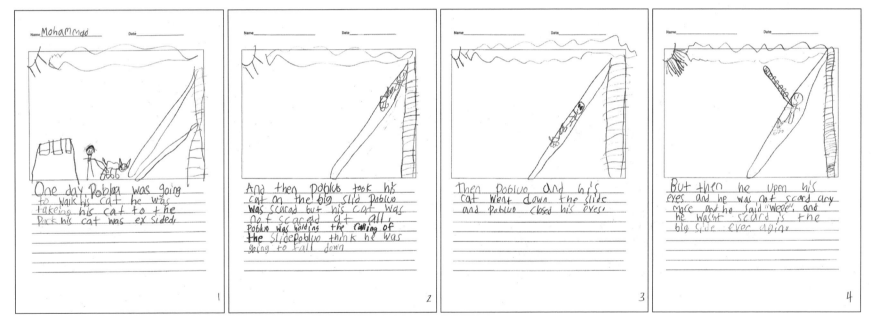

Page 1: One day Pablo was going to walk his cat. He was taking his cat to the park. His cat was excited.

Page 2: And then Pablo took his cat on the big slide. Pablo was scared but his cat was not scared at all. Pablo was holding the railing of the slide. Pablo thinks he was going to fall down.

Page 3: Then Pablo and his cat went down the slide and Pablo closed his eyes.

Page 4: But then he opened his eyes and he was not scared any more. He said "wee." And he wasn't scared on the big slide ever again.

FIG. 2–1   Mohammad's piece shows one way he elaborated by using descriptive detail to show how his character felt and adding what his character thought.

So I said, "Okay, remember how we said you can pretend to be the character. I bet you could give that a try. Let's become Pablo. You can look at your picture and show me with your body what Pablo looks like in this part of the story when he was scared on the slide."

Mohammad scrunched his face and clenched his fists, gesturing holding tightly on the rail of the slide.

"Wow, I love the way you acted out your character. I can tell how scared he was just by looking at you. Now I bet you can try adding words to your writing so your readers will know too."

Mohammad said, "I can add, 'Pablo was holding the railing of the slide. He thinks he is going to fall down.'" He added that to page 2.

I gave one last affirmation, reinforcing the work he was now doing. "Acting out and becoming the character really helped you add more words. Are you going to add more to lots of your other pages now too?"

Developing Familiar Settings with Remembered Details

Play up the importance of setting, showing children how to use the details of a familiar place as their setting.

I motioned for children to gather in the meeting area, and waited for them to settle with their folders, as usual. "Writers, I want to give you a tip. The tip is about the place, or setting, in your fiction books. Even when you create pretend characters, you can put them in a favorite place. Like a favorite playground or your street. When you do that, it helps you put in lots of details about the place, because you know it so well. You just close your eyes, imagine it, and then add the details before you forget. Alejandra has put her pretend character into a place she knows well: the park. (see Figure 2–2).

"Let me show you how Alejandra did this. Alejandra rehearsed her story and it started like this. 'Gilda was running to the park with her sister. Gilda just loved the park.' Then Alejandra told her partner about the park, and how much she loved the flowers and the sunlight there. You know what her partner said? She said, 'Put that in! The stuff about the flowers and the sunlight!'"

I picked up Alejandra's piece. "Listen to what Alejandra wrote, once she really thought about and remembered the details of this park she loves." I read, "'One day Gilda was running to the park with her sister. Gilda felt so refreshed in the breeze and in the sun light. Gilda also liked to smell the flowers.'

"Isn't that great, children? Alejandra really brought her setting alive, because she used details she really remembered. Will you do this now? Will you take out the story you are writing?" I waited a moment. "Now, will you really picture one place in your story—a place you can really imagine in detail, including what it sounds like, feels like, smells like? Close your eyes, really picture it. Put a thumb up when you have some details in your mind." I waited another moment. "Now, partners, tell each other some of those details." I let them talk for a minute, then interrupted. "Writers, one last tip. You have these details in your mind—now you'll want to get them on the page. Think for a moment—do you need to get some paper and staple it in, to add a whole page about your setting? Can you add in some sentences on the pages that are there? Let's do this important work now. Get some of these details into your story while they're fresh in your mind."

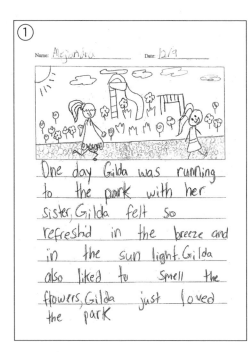

① One day Gilda was running to the park with her sister, Gilda felt so refreshd in the breeze and in the sun light. Gilda also liked to smell the flowers, Gilda just loved the park

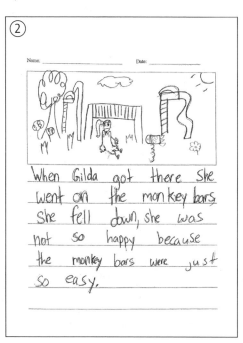

② When Gilda got there she went on the monkey bars, she fell down, she was not so happy because the monkey bars were just so easy.

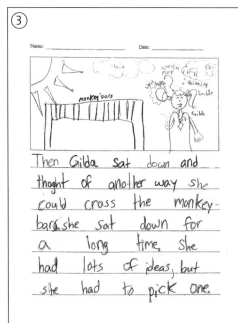

③ Then Gilda sat down and thoght of another way she could cross the monkey-bars she sat down for a long time, she had lots of ideas, but she had to pick one.

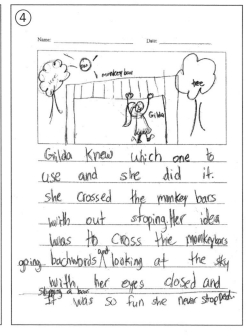

④ Gilda knew which one to use and she did it. she crossed the monkey bars with out stoping. Her idea was to cross the monkeybars going bachwords and looking at the sky with her eyes closed and skipping a bar It was so fun she never stopped.

One day Gilda was running to the park with her sister. Gilda felt so refreshed in the breeze and in the sun light. Gilda also liked to smell the flowers. Gilda just loved the park. When Gilda got there she went on the monkey bars, she fell down, she was not happy because the monkey bars were just so easy. Then Gilda sat down and thought of another way she could cross the monkey bars. She sat down for a long time. She had lots of ideas, but she had to pick one. Gilda knew which one to use and she did it. She crossed the monkey bars without stopping. Her idea was to cross the monkey bars going backwards and looking at the sky with her eyes closed and skipping a bar. It was so fun she never stopped.

FIG. 2–2 This piece shows a young writer stretching her story across pages. One way she elaborates is to add realistic, remembered details about her setting—a park the writer knew well.

Writers Learn to Get Their Characters Out of Trouble

BY NOW YOUR WRITERS will have two, three, or even four stories. Some of these stories will be "done," and others may still need endings. Even the ones that end may not actually have any kind of ending that we recognize. It's somewhat mysterious what leads kids to say that a story is done. Sometimes they seem completely at ease ending the story before anything has actually happened. Other times they end it with a cliffhanger. Their sense of logic is not ours.

This seems true even when students have been read to a lot. It's rare to find a children's story that doesn't have a problem-solution structure. *Harry the Dirty Dog*, *The Paper Bag Princess*, *Ferdinand the Bull*, *Mr. Putter and Tabby*—they all circle around a problem that gets resolved. And yet six- and seven-year-olds resist this logic in their own writing.

You've done some work now on structure, teaching children that they can develop some trouble the character gets into and then think about how the character will get out of that trouble. What often happens, though, is that children elaborate the beginning of a story, and the middle of a story, but they rarely stretch out the ending.

To elaborate on the ending, it's often helpful to think about "endings" rather than "the end." An ending implies that something happens—there is action or dialogue or the character feels something (all part of the narrative learning progression for first grade). In this session, you'll narrow the focus to what happens to the characters at the end of the story, with the aim of teaching your writers to get their characters out of trouble. This work will help them meet and go beyond the Common Core expectations for first-grade narrative writers, where they are expected to "provide some sense of closure" (W.1.3). The children will also have an opportunity to practice their close reading skills, as they study your exemplar text for evidence of details such as action, dialogue, and feelings. You'll model all of those, and your writers will probably try one. Really, though, the purpose of this lesson is to show kids how to stretch out a part of their story with detail. In this session you will show how to do that as revision, but you will want kids to know that this is something that they can do as they draft or as they revise their stories.

IN THIS SESSION, you'll teach children that writers make endings that satisfy their reader; they make something happen through action, dialogue, or feeling to get their characters out of trouble.

GETTING READY

✔ A story that has a missing ending, leaving the kids wanting more or wanting an ending. The story used here originates in the narrative learning progression exemplars (see Connection).

✔ Two versions of a story about your own character from Session 1, one without a satisfying ending, which you'll read aloud, and one with a good ending to show your revision! (see Teaching)

✔ "Ways to Bring Stories to Life" chart from Unit 1, *Small Moments*. You may want to pull it from the wall and bring it front and center during the minilesson (see Teaching).

✔ Paper and tape on hand (see Share)

COMMON CORE STATE STANDARDS: W.1.3, W.2.3, RL.1.1, RL.1.3, RL.2.3, SL.1.1, SL.1.4, L.1.1, L.1.2

Writers Learn to Get Their Characters Out of Trouble

CONNECTION

Tell a story that has a missing ending, leaving your students wanting more.

"Come close, children, I have a story to tell you. It's a little scary, so come in nice and close with your partner." I waited until they were leaning in, eyes big.

"Sarah and Julie were walking to school. It was Julie's first day of kindergarten. Her big sister, Sarah, was going to keep her safe on the way to school. 'Bye!' they shouted, as they left the house. 'This is great!' Julie said as they walked down the block. The sun was shining. The flowers were out. They turned the corner." I made my voice low and full of tension. The kids leaned in even closer. "That's when they saw it. They saw . . . "

I stopped and sat up. The kids, of course, whispered, "What? What did they see?"

"Wouldn't it be mean if I ended the story there, readers? If I just said, 'They saw . . . *the end!*' You want to know what happens next, right?"

The children nodded fiercely.

❖ Name the teaching point.

"Writers, today I want to teach you that readers love satisfying endings. One way writers create satisfying endings for their readers is by telling what happens to their characters at the end of their story. This makes their readers happy!"

TEACHING

Show students that they can make something happen to their character. Demonstrate with your own story that has a missing ending, leaving the reader feeling unsatisfied. Then offer choices about what could happen to the character that would satisfy the reader.

"Writers, I'm just finishing a Gretchen story. I'm going to share the way the story ends right now. Can you give me a huge thumbs up if you like the ending, and a thumbs down if you don't and think I should revise it? Thumbs up for a satisfying ending—it makes you happy because you know what happened. Thumbs down if it doesn't."

◆ COACHING

Storytelling is a key element of engagement. Learn to be a dramatic storyteller, and you'll never struggle to hold your children's attention.

This kind of mini-drama, an enactment of an actual story, makes your point better than any amount of explanation. To parallel this work in reading, when you're reading aloud, you might sometimes pause and ask, "Could that be the ending?" just when it's at a cliffhanger moment.

I picked up my booklet, ready to read. First, I retold the story so far. "This is a story where Gretchen got stuck in the tree house in a thunderstorm. Gretchen was in her tree fort when it began to thunder. She couldn't decide whether to stay in the tree fort or run for the house. Then lightning came, close! This is where I want to work on the ending. Listen to this ending. Thumbs up, or thumbs down?

> Lightning flashed. Gretchen trembled. "Mommy!" she yelled. No one came. Then suddenly . . . a
> bigger flash! CRACK!

"Thumbs up or thumbs down, writers? Does it seem like I fixed the trouble? Are you satisfied?" Thumbs turned down everywhere.

"Hmm . . . the way that story ended didn't seem so good! Maybe it's because Gretchen was still stuck in the tree fort."

I put down the booklet. "I should try to get my character out of trouble. I need to make sure that I fix the trouble she is in. Watch me try that. Watch as I revise the ending." I looked at my booklet and then stared into space. On the chart paper I wrote:

> Gretchen hid her head in her hands. CRACK! She was cold. Then the storm passed. Gretchen's
> mom yelled, "Gretchen, come inside and get dry. I made hot chocolate!" Gretchen climbed down
> the tree house. She felt safe at last!

I looked up. "Thumbs up or down?" Thumbs flashed up. "You feel better, right?" I asked. "It's because now something happens at the end, to my character. Writers, you can make your readers happy too, by getting your character out of trouble."

I pointed back to the chart paper with my exemplar ending and picked up a marker to add to the chart. "Here's a tip for writing endings that make readers happy. First and most important—write a solution! Get your character out of trouble!" In big red letters I added to the chart, above my ending, "Fiction Writers Get Their Character Out of Trouble!"

"Another tip is that everything you learned about bringing stories to life in small moments works for when you want to stretch out the ending of your story too. Remember when you learned to make people move or talk, and to feel and think?" I pointed to the "Ways to Bring Stories to Life" chart from *Small Moments*, which I had moved to the front of the room before the minilesson. "Well, you can do the same thing in your endings. You can add action by telling what the character did; dialogue by telling what the character said; or feelings by telling how the character felt.

"Look, see if you find evidence of those in my ending." I said them again, "Action . . . dialogue . . . feelings. Quick, work with your partner. Do you see evidence of any of these?" After just a moment I interrupted. "I saw you pointing out the action here," I pointed and annotated the ending as I spoke, "the dialogue here, and feelings here!"

"Let's keep this example up, to help us." I moved the chart to the side.

This chart will serve as a reminder of prior teaching.

① Gretchen hid her head in her hands. Crack! She was cold.

② Then the storm passed. Gretchen's mom yelled, "Gretchen, come inside and get dry. I made hot chocolate.

③ Gretchen climbed down the tree house.

④ She felt safe at last.

FIG. 3–1 Once again, the teacher's demonstration text will be an important scaffold in the room, not only during the minilesson but also as a cuing system for children to turn to when they need a familiar mentor.

Fiction Writers Get Their Character Out of Trouble!

Gretchen hid her head in her hands. CRACK! She was wet and cold. Then the storm passed.
Gretchen's mom yelled, "Gretchen, come inside and get dry. I made hot chocolate!" [DIALOGUE]
Gretchen climbed down the tree house. [ACTION] She felt safe at last! [FEELINGS]

ACTIVE ENGAGEMENT

Invite students to create other endings for the story you told. Remind them to get the character out of trouble.

"Writers, let's give you a chance to try this. There's no one way to end a story. In fact, writers often try more than one ending. Let's go back to my story again and imagine some other endings. Remember your tips—get your character out of trouble! And to stretch out the ending, you can use action, dialogue, or feelings."

I retold my story. "Gretchen was in the tree fort when it began to thunder. She couldn't decide whether to stay in the tree fort or run for the house. Then lightning came, close!

"Writers, I'm going to give you a chance to work on revising the ending with your partner. If you were going to get Gretchen out of trouble, what might you do? Go ahead. Give it a try. I'll listen in."

Listen in as the kids give it a try, and then retell some of their endings, illustrating that there is no one perfect ending but that writers work hard on their endings and make choices.

"Eyes up here, writers. I heard some endings that would make me really satisfied as a reader! Annabel and Miles came up with this ending: 'Gretchen scrambled down the ladder. Gretchen raced for the house. Her mom was in the door. She ran fast. Phew! She was safe!' That ending gets Gretchen out of trouble with a lot of action! Elisa and David said, 'Gretchen hid in the corner of the tree fort. The branches overhead kept her dry. 'This is fun,' Gretchen thought. Soon the storm was over.' That ending included what Gretchen thought. I love these endings, writers—they really get Gretchen out of trouble. I'll have to think about which ending I like best for my story—I have a lot to choose from."

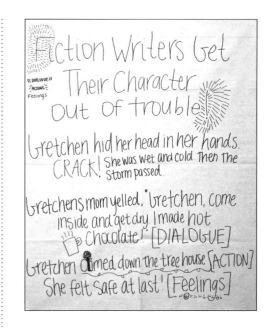

Gretchen raced for the house. Her mom was in the door. She ran fast.

FIG. 3–2 Stretching out the ending can provide more closure to a story—as well as added drama!

By having the children rehearse a different ending than the one they just heard, you also implicitly reinforce the notion that writers experiment—they try things more than one way. If you play up that skill, your children may follow suit.

Restate the steps your students just followed, so kids can follow the same process when they give it a try on their own stories. Tuck in the tip about using dialogue, action, or feelings to make something happen.

I paused. "Writers, let's review the work you've just done, because it's very important. You learned that writers can go back into their stories and work on their endings. One way they can work on their endings is to get their character out of trouble. A special tip you learned was if you use dialogue or action or feelings, it helps you stretch out the ending. What's important is that you know you can go back into your stories and elaborate on them—even when you thought they were done!"

LINK

Send the children off, taking the opportunity to explain what it will look like as they go off to write.

"Writers, this is an important step you're taking today, which is to think about making your reader happy as you write—that means that you want to make sure you have an ending that satisfies your reader. You can do this in the story you are working on now, or you can look back and revise one of your endings to a story that you have finished. Whenever you are writing, you can add on and make it better. I'm going to admire you as you get started. I'm sure I'll see some of you finishing a story and some of you getting out the stories you already wrote and adding new pages to the endings. Remember, you can grab some tape, and add more pages or revision strips to your stories if you want to add on to them!"

In your link, you can refer to the choices writers might make. While it's more efficient to encourage them all to do one thing (usually what you just taught), independent writers need to learn to make effective choices.

Writing for the Reader

TODAY, AS YOU TAUGHT YOUR WRITERS TO STRETCH OUT THEIR ENDINGS, you emphasized that they do this work to satisfy a reader. Whenever we are reading silently in the presence of children, we let our bodies convey the sense of drama capturing us as readers. We grip the book tightly. We murmur, "Oh no!" Time and again, children will ask, "What? What? What's happening?" When we read aloud, we let our bodies *and* our voices respond to the narrative, bringing our voice to a whisper for tense moments, reading at speed for exciting parts.

Teaching children to read their own writing with this same sense of drama helps them as readers and writers. As readers, it helps their intonation. As writers, noticing the drama in their stories helps them go back and add on to their writing, especially when you highlight how writers use dialogue and action to create drama. You might, then, gather a partnership and show them how to read their stories with feeling and expression, and then show them that adding action or dialogue can make their stories even more dramatic.

You may say to your kids, "You can read the books you write the same way you read books from our library. Really listen for when the characters get in trouble—and make that very dramatic. Listen for the dialogue too—are people talking? Yelling? Make your voice capture that excitement. And if you want more excitement, add some dialogue or action." Partners can help each other read, reread with more drama, and add things into their writing to make it more dramatic.

Autumn, for instance, worked with her partner on reading her story about finding a slug. At one point in her story (see Figure 3–3 on page 28), she had written, "Tewac started to run away." She read that with drama. Then her partner said, "Maybe he could YELL something as he ran. That would make it even more exciting." After some consultation, the girls came up with, "Then Tewac started to run away and yelled I don't like slugs!" which Autumn read aloud with much drama.

"So the question to ask yourself," I said to Autumn, "is what can you do as a writer to really make sure the reader knows that Tewac is yelling? What clues can you give?" I asked. "I could use exclamation marks," Autumn said. I nodded. "Anything else?" I queried. "And I could make big letters," Autumn added. I left her to it.

MID-WORKSHOP TEACHING Trying More than One Ending and Using a Partner to Get Feedback

"Writers, can I stop you for a moment? Autumn and Annabel are doing some great work that I want to share with all of you. Annabel wrote *three* different endings to one of her stories! Isn't that amazing, that she would work that hard as a writer? That's going to take you far, Annabel. She has her three different endings on different pieces of paper. Now she and Autumn have put all three in front of them on the floor, and they're deciding together which ending they like the best. Isn't that a great way for partners to work together? You are *so* lucky to write with your friends." (See Figures 3–4 and 3–5.)

I held up Annabel's papers, put them back down again, and shook both of their hands, formally. "Well done, partners. I'd be honored to work with you sometime."

FIG. 3–3 Autumn's creative control of capitals and exclamation points leads her readers to read with greater emotion.

The man took Mary all over the aquarium. Then Mary saw her class. Mary said, "that's my class!" Mary's teacher said, "Where were you?" Mary said, "I was lost." Mary thought that I should pay attention to my class next time.

FIG. 3–4 Annabel works on her ending. This ending includes a moral, or lesson—something Annabel carries over from reading workshop!

Seyony said, "come on let's look at the snail." Rdecoy said, "Ok, I will try not to be scared."

FIG. 3–5 Autumn's use of dialogue in the ending to her story captures her character's emotions of being afraid of a slug.

Beginnings that Have Action, Dialogue, or Feelings

Draw parallels between how writers work on endings and how they work on beginnings. Remind students they can add onto their stories and share their work with their partner.

"Writers, pens down for a moment, please, and eyes up here." When all the children were looking up, I said, "Children, one of you just asked the most interesting question. The question was, 'Can I work on the beginning of my story again too? What if I want to use action, dialogue, or feelings at the beginning of a story?' Isn't that a good question? I bet you already are thinking that the answer is . . . " I paused until they were saying, "Yes!"

"Yes, writers go back and add on to the beginning of their stories as well. They look over their stories, and they think about the beginnings just as they thought about the endings. I'm thinking that at the beginning of my story about Gretchen, I should say more about Gretchen's feelings about storms—and maybe add in some dialogue or action rather than just saying she was cold. I think I'm going to write two extra pages and tape them into my 'Gretchen and the Big Storm' book.

"I'm sure you've got ideas for how to add on to your beginnings too. Right now, why don't you take out your stories." I waited as they did so. "Find one that you think you could add more to the beginning. Put your finger on the part you're thinking about." I waited again. "Could you add a whole page? Could you add some dialogue, or some action? Think for a moment about the action you could add . . . or characters talking . . . or what characters feel . . . " I waited. "Now, turn and tell your partner . . . what do you want to add?"

After they had talked for a few minutes, I motioned to the paper and tape at hand. "Writers, there are three important things you are doing that I'm hoping you'll keep doing as writers." I put my finger in the air. "One, you realized that when you learn to improve one part of your writing, you can do that work in any part of your writing. Two, you used your partner to rehearse the parts you wanted to add. That's always a good idea. And three, writers capture those words on paper while they're thinking of them. So there's tape and paper on hand. Go ahead, add some words to the pages you have, or add in a revision strip or a new page! And remember, the next time you start a new story, you can be thinking of the same things you're thinking about as you revise your stories—adding action, dialogue, or feelings for your character *as* you write.

Serious Writers Get
Serious about Spelling

IN THIS SESSION, you'll teach children that writers make coura-geous choices about words in their stories—they tackle sparkling words as they write. They also use everything they know about spelling to write these daring words.

GETTING READY

✔ List of "sparkle words" (challenging words) taken from your students' writing, to share with the class (see Connection)

✔ "Ways to Spell Words" chart from Unit 3, *Writing Reviews*. You may want to pull it from the wall and bring it front and center during the minilesson (see Teaching and Active Engagement).

✔ Your own demonstration text, using the same character from previous ses-sions, with sketches completed to show that you have planned it already

✔ At least two words selected from your story to demonstrate spelling strategies that your class needs. We use the words *splashing* and *twisted* (see Teaching and Active Engagement).

✔ White boards and dry erase markers for each child to use during the active engagement

COMMON CORE STATE STANDARDS: W.1.3, W.1.5, W.2.3, RFS.1.2, RFS.1.3, SL.1.1, SL.1.2, L.1.1, L.1.2.d,e; L.1.5, L.1.6

O NE THING I AM SURE YOU ARE HOPING TO SEE at this point in the year is evidence that all you have done in word study is being transferred to indepen-dent writing. You may see children working on various spelling patterns, long vowels, and short vowels during word study. Writing workshop gives your youngsters the opportunity to put these word study principles into practice. In fact, the more they write, the more practice they get using all the spelling strategies they are learning. While they're writ-ing, you'll see children make important and courageous choices about letters and patterns.

One crucial thing to remember with young writers is that you *want* them to use words they don't know how to spell yet. If they only use words they are sure about, they'll never be daring with their vocabulary. Praise your writers for being daring, celebrate their spar-kling words, and give them feedback on how to move closer to accurate spelling, all the while expecting that as seven-year-olds, of course they won't be accurate yet with lots of words. We're particularly speaking of non–high-frequency words here such as *terrible* and *scary* and *wonderful* and *surprising*—words kids use a lot in stories but that aren't ordinary social language or high-frequency words at their age.

As your kids are storytelling, you'll hear them use these literary words, and you'll be so pleased. Then you'll see their writing, and sometimes these words will be missing. This might mean they are afraid to use words they don't yet know how to spell, or they may get overwhelmed as they try to picture what the word looks like. The idea of attacking longer and unfamiliar words can seem daunting and overwhelming to them.

It would be a shame if a child said, "Max rode his bike down a dangerous hill," but on paper simply wrote, "Max rode his bike down a big hill" just because she knew how to spell the word *big* and not *dangerous*.

This session, then, addresses two writerly skills: using more sparkling, sophisticated vocabulary and working on spelling strategies. This lesson also reminds students that they don't need to wait until they are editing their fiction books to work on their spelling. They can use all they know about spelling to tackle tricky words as they draft their books. And remember, reward them for being brave!

Serious Writers Get Serious about Spelling

CONNECTION

Praise children for being daring writers, and celebrate their courage in choosing fancy words they don't yet know how to spell.

"Writers, gather around. I would like to start writing workshop today by giving you some feedback. Ready? Listen up." There was a dramatic pause, and I sat up straight and tall and said, "I am happy about your work! No . . . not just happy . . . proud. No, not just proud . . . *delighted*—that's the fancy word I'm looking for. I'm delighted at something you're doing." As I said this, the kids also began to sit up tall with their shoulders back, smiling. I acknowledged their change of body position and said, "And you can be proud of, no, *delighted* with yourselves too! Here's why: One of the daring things you are doing is you are being brave with your words. You are choosing a lot of fancy words like *frightening* and *awful* and *brilliant*. We might call these 'sparkle words.' It's so daring to write words you don't know how to spell yet. I love to see you do that. Go ahead, give your partner a high five right now, for daring to use sparkle words you didn't even know for sure how to spell!"

The children gave each other high fives happily. Then I continued, "Writers, look at this list of sparkle words. It is not just any old list. It is a list of words kids in *this* class have written. I pulled it from *your* stories! I know—pretty amazing!"

Sparkle Words

refreshed, backwards, aquarium, surprised, scrambled . . .

"Writers, I know this is just the start, and there will be more, so we can keep adding to it."

Remind children that they know a lot about spelling, and bring out a familiar chart that will cue up their repertoire of strategies.

"As fiction writers, I know there are lots of cool and fancy sparkle words you want to include in your writing—words you have never written before. So I was reminded of the chart we have to help you spell." I then gestured to the "Ways to Spell Words" chart, which I pulled down from the wall so it would be close by during the lesson.

You might want to come up with classroom lingo for these kinds of words, such as sparkle words *or* daring words, *to emphasize the courage and sophistication it takes to tackle challenging words in their writing.*

"Then I realized, writers, you're not only daring. You're also pretty expert. You know a lot about spelling by now. So you can use all you know to write any word you want!"

❖ Name the teaching point.

"Today I want to teach you that writers often choose special and fancy words to bring sparkle to their stories. These daring writers remember and use all they know about spelling as they write."

TEACHING

Role-play being a writer their age who is daring to use sparkling words.

"Writers, I want to give this a try. Right now, I am going to pretend I am a *first-grader* writing a fiction book just like you. And I want to write sparkle words to make my story come to life. Watch what I do."

I waited until all eyes were on me, expectant. "Okay, I am writing a story about my character Gretchen. It's about an adventure Gretchen has at the beach, where it is her first time on a boogie board. I already did my sketches, and now I am ready to write the words. I want to write that Gretchen was 'splashing in the waves.'"

Continue your role play, putting into play all the spelling strategies children have learned so far.

"Hmm, but *splashing* seems like a huge word. What shall I do? If I don't know how to spell it, I guess I could leave it out!" I looked woebegone. Then I sat up straight, exaggerating my use of the strategies on the class chart. "Oh no, that's right. I can be daring and spell the word the best I can. I can look closely at the chart to remind myself of everything I know about how to spell. Let's see. Let me say it. Spl - a - sh - ing." I slowed my voice down and repeated it several times. Children were mouthing it as well.

"I am not going to listen for just the first letter because I know I can listen to parts of words." I pointed to "Write it part by part" on the chart. "So the first part I hear is *spl*. Hmm, not just /s/. I hear a blend of /spl/. Three letters." I jotted those three letters. "Now let me say it again. Splashing. Oh, I hear /a/ like in *apple*." I said it again, emphasizing the short *a* and then added "a." Then I said the word again. "Spl - a - sh. Hey, wait! That is those two letters that make that one sound: *sh*!" I added the letters to the word. Then I said the whole word, slowly, again. "Spl - a - sh - ing!" I repeated /ing/ again slowly.

I looked at the chart, pointing to using words you know. "Oh, I know that from another word. I have written that before." I added "ing" to the end of the word. Now I have all of it!" I looked up, as if excited and pleased.

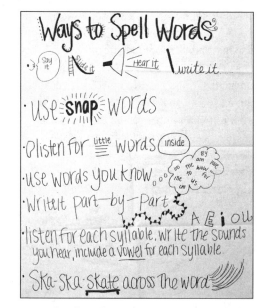

Using familiar charts in new situations teaches children to use the tools at hand to raise the level of their work.

Recap what you just did as a process they can follow as well. Play up the sense of achievement.

"Wow, I used lots of spelling strategies to help me write this one word. *And* it really did help. Did you see how I thought about all the parts of the word, saying it over and over again, and when I felt stuck I looked at the chart to see if it could help me spell this daring sparkle word?"

ACTIVE ENGAGEMENT

Using classroom tools such as white boards, give children a chance to work on a word from your story, using all they know about spelling.

I quickly made sure each child had a white board and marker. "So, writers, can you help me with another word in my story? In my story Gretchen runs out of the water and falls down. I could just write that she *fell*. That would be easy because I know how to spell *fell*. I've written that word a bunch of times. But I want my reader to know that she ran so fast she *twisted* her foot. So, can you all help me out with the word *twisted*?"

The children nodded. On the chart I wrote:

Gretchen ran so fast she _____ her foot.

"Everyone, take a look at the spelling chart, and work on this word for a bit using your white board. Use all you know to write the word *twisted*. You can compare with your partner. It's a daring sparkle word!"

Voice over the strategies you are hoping kids will use. Praise perseverance.

I voiced over strategies I saw kids using, or ones I hoped they would use. "Oh, I see Nandika and her partner have discovered the /tw/ blend! I love how they kept repeating the first part of the word until they were pretty sure it was *tw*!" And "Robert has just figured out the short *i* sound after several tries! Nicely done. That was tricky!"

Share the accurate spelling. Remind students that it's not about achieving accuracy with every sparkle word. It's about using all the spelling strategies they know to work hard and independently.

When I had a sense that most children had worked across the sounds of the word, I wrote the correct spelling of the word on the chart. Partners immediately began to check their spelling against *twisted*. "Writers, I see that many of you got close to the spelling of this sparkle word, and some of you even got all the letters right. Don't worry if it isn't perfect. Working hard and using everything you know is what's important."

Reiterating the steps you follow is very helpful as children learn a new process, not just a strategy.

You won't want to wait until every last writer has finished sounding out and recording the word, but you will want to give children enough time that most of them have finished making their predictions. Asking them to share with their partners will help along your writers who need extra support sounding out words. And emphasizing working hard—over the correct answer—will fuel their energy for working on spelling sparkle words in their own writing.

LINK

As you send children off to write, empower them to make choices as writers.

"Children, daring writers choose sparkle words whenever they write, and they won't always know how to spell them. So they use everything they know about spelling to do the best they can. I'm going to admire you now as you go off to write. I bet I'll see some of you going back to your stories to work on some of those sparkle words. And I bet I'll see a lot of you working on your spelling as you write daring words in your new writing today. Maybe I'll even see you and your partner studying our chart together and working together to help each other. Call me over if you do some work you're especially proud of, okay?"

Knowing the Developmental Spelling Stages of Your Writers

IN TODAY'S CONFERENCES AND SMALL GROUPS, you might want to focus on supporting students with their spelling and conventions to match the work of the minilesson. Kids don't tend to develop control of spelling patterns or conventions at the same time, which means you pretty much always need to differentiate this instruction. It is important that you know the spelling stages of your students. (We tend to use Donald Bear's *Words Their Way* (2011) as a spelling curriculum, and classes are generally broken into three to five different levels, or stages.) This will make it easier to teach some small groups that are specifically geared to the type of spelling strategies they are ready for. Undoubtedly, you will have kids at various stages of spelling development. You may decide to pull a small group that is behind and one that is ahead. Regardless of the specific focus of your groups, one thing you may decide to emphasize is that writers don't wait for an editing day to spend a little time on spelling or to fix up words that don't look right. They also do it as they write!

You might also decide to focus on spelling in your one-to-one conferences today, as I did with Zahir. I pulled up next to Zahir as he was writing the word *snail*. I noticed he was saying it slowly to get it on paper. I waited to observe what he would do. He wrote the letters *sailn*. I was pleased he remembered the *ai* spelling pattern, which we had done in word study. That clearly was something to compliment. I was also surprised he missed the *sn* blend at the beginning and ended with the *n*. That suggested he heard the *n*, but just put it out of order.

Data in hand, and sure that Zahir could do better, I decided to stop him at this point to teach him to reread and fix it on the run rather than waiting for later editing.

I gave Zahir the compliment of hearing the *ai* spelling pattern and then added, "Reread the word closely. Does it look right?"

Zahir looked puzzled. I said, "Say the word again and listen carefully to the ending. What sound do you hear at the end?"

Zahir immediately knew it was an *l* sound and not the *n* and started erasing the final *n* he had written. So I said, "You were right about the *n* sound being somewhere in this word, you just have to say to yourself, 'Where does it go?' Say the word again, and you'll probably hear it."

Zahir then heard the *sn* consonant blend and added it in. I finished by restating the work we did, reminding him to say tricky words a few times and to be extra alert to endings as he writes more sparkle words.

(continues)

MID-WORKSHOP TEACHING **Highlight Work a Student Has Done in Rereading and Revising**

"Writers, let me stop you. I just noticed Heather do something so important. She was rereading her writing to see if it made sense and she noticed that sometimes how she spelled a word affected if her story made sense. Her story is about a birthday party and having yummy cake. When she reread the sentence she read, 'They ate yummy cak!'" Heather and I giggled. "Heather said, 'Cak. That is not a word!' Then she remembered that sometimes words have a silent marker to make the vowel say its name, and she added the silent *e*. Now it says *cake*!"

I looked around the room to be sure writers were paying attention. Then I held up two fingers. "Writers, Heather did two important things that you can all do. One, you can all reread your writing aloud to make sure it sounds right and will make sense to your readers. You might find a few things to fix up! Two, as you do that, you can think about if a word looks right to help the reader read the words more easily."

I then moved on to another child, keeping my focus today on spelling and conventions. I sat next to Nora and read her piece over her shoulder. I didn't want to waste time having her read it to me while I researched. So I read it and made the decision to jump right in with her, focusing on spelling a multisyllabic word, which can be a challenge for anyone.

I noticed the word *together* was spelled *tgthr* in her writing. So I complimented her attempt at a sparkle word and taught her to clap out each syllable and to write one syllable at a time. She then wrote *togthr*. Doing that helped her add the *o*. Next, I gave her a tip. I reminded her that each clap, or syllable, needs a vowel, and I pointed to that part of our "Ways to Spell Words" chart. We named the vowels together as a reminder. So, after that coaching, Nora wrote *togethur*. It was so close that I just told her it is actually an *er* not a *ur*, and then I acknowledged her brave and daring spelling.

Working Hard to Get to the Correct Spelling

Celebrate writers' spelling efforts, and teach students that they can go back and check their spelling of tricky words by writing them three ways and choosing the one that looks right or seems most familiar.

"Writers, today as you come to the meeting area please bring your writing and a pencil, and sit next to your writing partner." I waited until all the children were gathered. "I noticed you all worked so hard on your spelling today, so I thought you could do a couple of things with your partners to keep the good work going. So, the first thing is, show your partner a sparkle word you worked on today *and* teach him or her what you did to spell it. You can refer to the spelling chart to help you remember."

I gave them time to turn and talk, and I listened in to get ideas of kids to spotlight. Then I said, "Wow! Serenity added the word *quickly*. And Robert added the word *grabbed*. They used their spelling strategies to be daring.

"Okay, now ready for the next part? I want to make sure you know one of the most useful spelling strategies. It's one even adults use. Ready?

"You can reread your writing, choose a tricky word, and write it three times with different spellings. When you do this, you can then circle the one that is closest to the real spelling, especially if you've seen the word before. Give it a try. Reread your writing from today and choose a word that doesn't look quite right. Then, with your partner, write the word three times and together decide which one looks the best and circle it. Usually trying a few times helps us to see which one looks best. Write until it starts to look like the word you read in your books."

Gretchen ran so fast
She twisted twisted her
foot.
 x twistad
 x twisteed
 twisted
 √ twisted !!!!

FIG. 4–1 Children try different spellings of difficult words.

Taking Stock
Writers Use Checklists to Set Goals

IN THIS SESSION, you'll teach students that writers use checklists to review their writing and set goals.

GETTING READY

✔ Narrative Writing Checklists, Grades 1 and 2, chart-sized and small copies for students (see Guided Inquiry)

✔ Your own demonstration text to model using the checklist. You'll want to use a story from the character you introduced in Session 1—for example, "Gretchen Finds a Baby Raccoon."

✔ Class set of Post-its (two different colors, for example, green and red) and markers

✔ Small cards for students to write their goals on (see Guided Inquiry)

Y OUR WRITERS HAVE DONE A LOT of important writing work so far, extending their narrative powers, as well as their fluency and stamina. They have a repertoire of things they could be working on now as writers. Mostly, children have been inspired to add on, and now to revise, by focusing on parts of texts. Today, you'll move children to assess where they are holistically as writers. What you'll really want them to do is to think not just about the piece in front of them, but about themselves as writers. Partway through a unit of study, when children have put in some serious effort yet still have plenty of time to get even better, is a great time for this kind of self-assessment.

One of the tools that can help children's assessment be more specific rather than general is a specific, calibrated checklist. In this session, you'll ask your students to return to the Narrative Writing Checklist they were introduced to in the beginning of the year during the *Small Moments* unit, to review their strengths and set new overall goals as writers.

Even as you scaffold this process (which you'll have to do, because there are simply too many important steps to send them off on their own), you'll want to act as if your children remember this process from using checklists during persuasive writing and earlier in the year. That is, you don't want to teach something that is *not* new as if it is new. Rather, you'll want to reinforce and extend. Of course, if you think your kids are ready to use the checklist independently, set goals, and organize themselves to work on these goals, go ahead and let them get started, and just give them some feedback and tips. This session, though, provides concrete scaffolds.

It's amazing how much "swag" pleases all of us. Having on hand special Post-its, highlighters, or colored stickers really energizes children's work with checklists. There is also something tactile about being able to put a sticker on the place in their writing (the evidence) that proves they did something on the checklist.

Taking Stock
Writers Use Checklists to Set Goals

CONNECTION

Tell writers that instead of a regular minilesson, they'll inquire into ways they can and cannot yet do all that is expected of first-grade storytellers (narrative writers) at the end of the year.

"Writers, you've been working hard as fiction writers now for awhile, and you have important choices to make each day as you decide what to work on."

I looked at the children seriously, one writer to another. "It's sort of a big deal for writers, deciding what to do each day. You might decide to do things in your book that you see your partner or your classmates doing, for instance. You might add important details to your story. You might work hard at your endings. And those are just some of the new things you've been working on. You already knew about writing small moments, about making characters talk, about using capitals and punctuation to help your reader, and so much more.

"So today I was thinking that instead of a regular minilesson, I could help you try to make expert decisions about your big, personal goals as a writer. One way to do this is to evaluate the fiction book you think is your best so far. That way, you can figure out the things that you do well and compliment yourself on those things, and figure out the things you want to work on, so you can set expert goals. And maybe, with help from your partner or classmates, you could do some big work on one of your personal goals today.

"This means that today we'll start with a minilesson where *you teach yourselves*. I think you'll remember how to do this once we get started."

GUIDED INQUIRY

Name a question that will guide the inquiry.

"Writers, today each of you is going to investigate the question, 'What am I doing well as a narrative writer, and what do I want to work on next?'"

◆ COACHING

Because it's later in the year, you'll have some students who may be ready for the second-grade checklist—so before starting this lesson, it makes sense to look across your student work and see which checklist you want to begin with. You'll know that it makes sense to bring out the second-grade checklist when you look at student writing and feel as if they are accomplishing the first-grade standards. That's a moment to pat yourself on the back, and simultaneously say "onward!" Rather than say "good job," and act as if these writers are done, you want to push these writers toward next steps and more ambitious goals. The second-grade checklist will help with that work. Later in the unit, in Session 10, students will have another opportunity to work with the checklist. You might even make it a goal that by then, most of your students will be ready to work with the second-grade list.

Set writers up to evaluate their writing by following a process to help them develop ways to compliment themselves and set important goals for next steps.

"So, writers, you probably remember how to do this. First, you put your best fiction book in front of you. You'll find some Post-its in your writing folder: green ones (remember, for go!) and red ones (remember, for stop!). Then you compare your writing with the Narrative Writing Checklist. You'll remember this list from our *Small Moments* unit at the beginning of the year. This is the list of things that writing teachers decided all first-graders should be able to do by the very end of first grade. It's getting close to the end of first grade, so when you decide what your next steps are as a writer, it's really important to make sure you've accomplished all of these goals. Today, we'll begin by checking these, and making plans to meet these goals right away. And if you feel good about those goals, I have the *second*-grade checklist for you!" (These checklists are available on the CD-ROM.)

"I've seen your fiction books, so I know that when you listen to this list, you'll say 'Hey, I'm doing that, right here, in this story!'"

Narrative Writing Checklist

	Grade 1	NOT YET	STARTING TO	YES!	Grade 2	NOT YET	STARTING TO	YES!
	Structure				**Structure**			
Overall	I wrote about when I did something.	☐	☐	☐	I wrote about *one time* when I did something.	☐	☐	☐
Lead	I tried to make a beginning for my story.	☐	☐	☐	I thought about how to write a good beginning and chose a way to start my story. I chose the action, talk, or setting that would make a good beginning.	☐	☐	☐
Transitions	I put my pages in order. I used words such as *and* and *then, so.*	☐	☐	☐	I told the story in order by using words such as *when, then, and after.*	☐	☐	☐
Ending	I found a way to end my story.	☐	☐	☐	I chose the action, talk, or feeling that would make a good ending.	☐	☐	☐
Organization	I wrote my story across three or more pages.	☐	☐	☐	I wrote a lot of lines on a page and wrote across a lot of pages.	☐	☐	☐
	Development				**Development**			
Elaboration	I put the picture from my mind onto the page. I had details in pictures and words.	☐	☐	☐	I tried to bring my characters to life with details, talk, and actions.	☐	☐	☐
Craft	I used labels and words to give details.	☐	☐	☐	I chose strong words that would help readers picture my story.	☐	☐	☐
	Language Conventions				**Language Conventions**			
Spelling	I used all I knew about words and chunks of words (*at, op, it*, etc.) to help me spell.	☐	☐	☐	To spell a word, I used what I knew about spelling patterns (*tion, er, ly*, etc.).	☐	☐	☐
	I spelled all the word wall words right and used the word wall to help me spell other words.	☐	☐	☐	I spelled all of the word wall words correctly and used the word wall to help me figure out how to spell other words.	☐	☐	☐

Scaffold students' self-evaluation by reading aloud the items under the first heading of the first-grade Narrative Writing Checklist.

Checklist in hand, I read the first item and said, "When you were writing Small Moment stories, you were writing about yourself. Now that you are writing fiction books, you are writing about something *your character* did. The trick is to write one small moment, about just one thing that happened—not *everything* or the character's *whole life*. That really is a second-grade goal that I think you're all ready to do. If you wrote about one time when your character did something, put a green Post-it on your first page, and write 'one time' on it." I demonstrated doing so.

Just as with prior experiences, you'll read the list, item by item, sometimes elaborating on an item and often coaching children in ways to use Post-its to note examples of that item. Often acting as if children will fulfill your extremely high expectations leads them closer to reaching your lofty goals. If a few of your children take a long time to jot Post-its, you could have some that are prewritten, at hand for them. The narrative checklist is angled toward personal narrative (I wrote about when I did something). Substitute "the character" for "I" to angle it toward fiction.

After reading second item, I said, "Did you work on a beginning? If you wrote a beginning that introduces the trouble in your story, put a green Post-it on that page, and write, 'beginning,' on it. I'm not sure I introduce the trouble in my story in the beginning, so I'm going to put a red Post-it on mine. I think I could do even better at beginnings.

After the third item, "I put my pages in order. I used words such as *and* and *then, so*," I said, "Remember how you worked on telling your story across your fingers? Do you connect these parts by using phrases like *first . . . then* or *the next day . . . later* to tell your reader that the story is moving along? If you did, put a Post-it on the page where you used these connecting words. Maybe write one of the words on the Post-it."

Reading the fourth item, I said, "I found a way to end my story." My ending is satisfying. Something happens, I got the character out of trouble. If you think your ending is your best writing, put a green Post-it there, and write 'end' on it. If you think you could do even better, put a red Post-it on the last page." I kept going then, with the last item under "Structure."

Encourage students to find evidence of their strengths in more than one fiction book.

"Writers, tell each other what you do well!" I said, and listened in for a minute. "Now prove it. Show your partner where your Post-it is, and give your partner proof!"

I gave them a minute to show off. "Listen, writers. What matters is not that you can do one of these things in one book. What's important is that you do this all the time as a writer. Now take one of the things you said you're good at and find evidence that you did this good writing work, in other fiction books you've written so far. Once you've found some places, show your partner. Really show off, so you'll know it's not just this one story. It's you as a writer."

The children dove into their books, putting fresh Post-its on pages, showing their work proudly to their partners. For some, it was hard to find more evidence of some work in earlier books.

Coach children to listen not only for what they already do well, but also for what they want to do even better, setting goals for themselves.

"Writers, many of you are finding that you did lots of things already in your writing, and that is great. But to become a much better writer, you also need to be hard on yourself and to be able to say, 'I can do more. I could be even better at this.' So let me reread the list we've gone through so far and ask you to think, 'Which of these things could I be *even better* at?' Then you will have time to tell your partner what your goals will be for the next part of our unit, for the next week or two. So listen up, and think, 'Which of those things could I be better at?'"

I reread the list and then said, "I know you'll want to talk to your partner about this important work. Go ahead and tell your partner which of these could become your own personal goals." After children talked for a bit, I gave each child a card and asked them to record a big, personal goal or two for themselves.

The goal here is exposure more than perfection. As you move down the list, you'll put Post-its on your own story to mark your evidence of an item and you'll give children time to scan through a page or two of their books in between items, but you won't wait for them each to be finished. It's not the checklist itself that is the goal, it's that writers realize there are grade-level expectations they are striving for. You are alerting them that, especially by this time in the year, they want to make sure they're reaching for and exceeding these specific expectations.

There's a difference between planning revision for an individual piece and setting big personal goals as a writer. These goals will be over-arching ones that children may strive to meet across several pieces. They'll also be helpful as the basis for your conferring, giving you a way to coach writers' ability to self-assess, to work toward goals, to realize when they are ready to outgrow them.

Repeat the process for the second two headings on the checklist, coaching children to listen not only for what they do well, but also to think about what their goals might be as writers.

"Writers, that was great. I especially admire those of you who decided that if you only did something one time, you still want to get even better at it. That is daring—to believe you can get *even better* at something, even if you sort of pulled it off one time." I said this even though they hadn't really done this, but now I saw kids nod and take in this advice.

"Writers, listen while I read the second two parts of this list, and choose one or two of these things you could do *more often*, and *even better*."

After rereading the second two parts of the checklist, I was silent while children recorded a goal or two.

"I am so proud of you for setting such daring goals. This is really going to let you be more independent. You just taught your own minilesson to yourself!"

Crystallize a few goals that many children seem to have identified, doing this in a way that reinforces these goals.

"Writers, let's take some bows. If you decided to get *even better* at beginnings, stand up and take a bow. Then look around at writers who set the same goal. Take note, because you'll want to sit near someone who has the same goal today." They did, gleefully.

"Okay, now if you decided to get even better at endings, take a bow and look around to see who shares your goal.

"Now if you set a goal of getting better at staying in one small moment, take a bow and notice your buddies.

"And finally, if one of your goals was getting better at connecting words, take a bow! See who you are? Very exciting."

LINK

Channel children to sit near other writers who are working on the same goal so they can help each other and show off their work.

"Now, writers, you're going to work independently, but this time, you'll sit near other writers who share one of your goals. That way, you can help each other, and you can show off your work.

"So for now, quickly decide which goal you'll be working on first today. Is it beginnings? Endings? Small moment? Connecting?"

I'd soon organized writers who wanted to work on one goal in one area of the classroom. Those who wanted to work on another goal were channeled to another area, and so on, often putting kids into partnerships to help them focus. "You are going to be writing right next to writers who share your goal, so you can help each other and also get ready to show off your work later, to someone who shares the same goal."

It would be easy for the children's work with a checklist to turn into a quick, glib, "checking" of boxes. Instead we emphasize how writers set high standards, asking themselves, "Is this my very best work, or could I do better?"

Giving children an opportunity to stand and move around really helps some of them get through the day successfully. Tom Newkirk, in Misreading Masculinity *(2002), encourages teachers to think of the active young male body and mind, and ensure school is congenial for these children.*

Reteaching the Minilesson to Reach Writers Who Need Support or Are Ready to Reach for Second-Grade Standards

IN YOUR CONFERRING SESSION, you may want to give some attention both to the writers who need extra support, and to the writers who are ready to reach for second-grade standards. For writers who need extra support, you might find, for example, that some kids have a difficult time managing a checklist and a folder full of stories. If so, then you may decide to start your conferring by pulling a small group to the meeting area and, using the same method of guided practice that was used in today's minilesson, repeat the process. You might even have Post-its that are prewritten, in both colors, so all they have to do is move them over, rather than jot on each. This time you will be able to guide at a slower pace and help kids name what they do well and an area they can work on. You may even decide to focus on fewer criteria and start them out with looking for only two items on the list.

Once they have managed to identify strengths and goals, you may want to confer by asking questions such as, "What are you trying to do today?" "How do you plan on doing that?" "Can you show me where you tried it?" "Have you tried doing it in more than one place or in more than one book?" "What do you plan to do next?" "Have you tried anything new today?"

Asking open-ended questions such as these will reinforce to students that they should feel daring and independent while you subtly provide some cues and set them up for their next work. Also, if you have decided to have your kids with common goals sit together, you will have instant small groups. The beauty of that is you can teach several children at once who are working on the same goal.

You'll also want to stay alert to your strong writers who need attention as well. If some of them have put green Post-its for virtually everything on the list, you might pull these writers into a group, and set them up with the second-grade narrative checklist. "I've been thinking about you as writers," you might say, "and I think that you're already ready to work toward some of the second-grade writing skills. In fact you may already be doing some of these things, though probably not in every story." Then read the list to them, giving them a chance to pull out their stories and show off places where they

approximated the work. Miles, for instance, pulled out his story about Six Flags (see Figure 5–1), which started:

> One spring day Chester was going to Six Flags. He is seven years old. It was really hot out. He was with his mom. He wanted to go on a ride. But then his mom said "Stop!" He stopped.

Working down the second-grade checklist, Miles showed off to his partner how he had set off his dialogue with quotation marks, how he stretched his story across a lot of pages, how he used connecting words like *later* and *finally*, and how he worked on an ending that even showed a lesson! Putting his finger on his last page, Miles read:

> Finally he stopped and went to the roller coaster and went on. He learned to not push his mom. He liked the roller coaster.

MID-WORKSHOP TEACHING
Writers Celebrate Each Other's Hard Work

"Writers, can I stop you for a moment? Let's not wait to celebrate some of the hard work you're doing! Take a second and see what you have done. Hold up your book if you revised your story to make sure you wrote about *one* time when your character did something. Okay, everyone, let's cheer hooray for them! Now, hold up your book if you used words like *and* and *then*. Okay, let's hear another hooray! Did anyone work on ending a story with action or dialogue? If so, hold it up. Wow! That's second-grade work. Hooray! Who else and what else? Hooray!"

You might finish by coaching students to tackle one of the second-grade goals together, setting up a meeting time for them to compare their writing. If these writers are also strong readers, you might point out particular mentor texts that might be right for their level. Your strongest writers need attention, in order to become extraordinary writers.

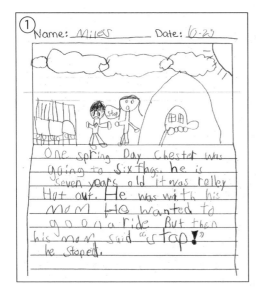

① Name: Miles   Date: 10-23

One spring Day Chester was going to Six Flags. he is seven years old it was relley Hot out. He was with his mom He wanted to go on a ride But then his mom said "stop!" he stoped.

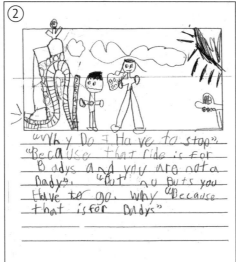

② "Why Do I Have to stop". "Because that ride is for Badys and you are not a Bady". "But you Buts you Have to go. Why "Because that is for Badys"

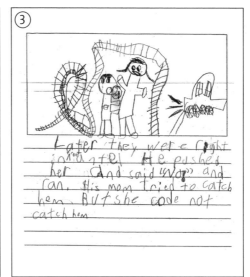

③ Later they were right in front of. He pushed her and said "Vo" and ran. His mom tried to catch him. But she code not catch him

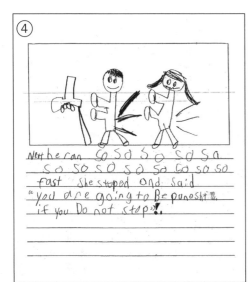

④ Next he ran so so so so so so so so so so so so so so fast She stoped and said "you are going to Be punosht if you Do not stop".

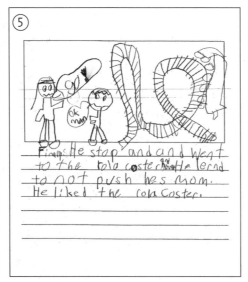

⑤ Finily He stop and and went to the rola coster and He lernd to not push hes mom. He liked the rola Coster.

FIG. 5–1 Miles reaches far beyond the second-grade standards, incorporating advanced language standards such as punctuation of dialogue, and advanced writing standards, such as including an ending that teaches a moral or lesson.

Celebrating Our Best Work

Invite children to celebrate their revision work by "sharing the mike."

"Children, sometimes at a celebration, there is this thing that happens that is called 'open microphone.' It's when someone gets up and takes the microphone and talks to the crowd about something he or she is really happy about. Here's your chance. Go back to your table with your writing. Look it over. When you find something you did that makes you really happy, ask for the mike and talk to the crowd about it! I know you all love to pretend, and we won't really have a microphone. You can simply hold your fist close to your mouth and act like you're talking into a real microphone." I demonstrated this, putting my fist in front of my mouth and saying, "Hello crowd! I'm here to celebrate my endings! I've really put a lot of work into them, and they are my pride and joy. Whoopee. Let's hear one of my endings . . .

I took my fist away. "Be dramatic! You know how singers look! Then you can share something wonderful about your writing. We'll work hard at sharing so we can hear from lots of you. If there are too many writers wanting to share all at once, we can stop, and you can use your partner. He or she is your best audience."

Soon you could hear the sounds of "open mike." "Hi, my name is Nora, and my best work is with dialogue—it's how I stretch out the trouble. Listen to this . . . 'The baby sister came in Rosa's room and messed up the painting and Rosa said, "Nooo!!!!" Then Rosa's Mom came and said, "What is going on?" and Rosa said, "My baby sister messed up my picture!"'" Nora took on the voices of her characters as she spoke into her "microphone." Her audience clapped for her, as around her others performed as well.

FIG. 5–2 Nora's third and fourth pages of her story show how she used dialogue to stretch out the trouble in her story.

Series Writers Always Have a Lot to Write About

IN THIS SESSION, you'll launch your writers into writing series, including thinking of more than one story for a favorite character and modeling themselves on famous series writers.

GETTING READY

✔ A variety of series books you and your class enjoy—for example, Henry and Mudge, Little Bill, Frog and Toad, Max and Ruby

✔ A boxed set to show children as an example of a series (see Teaching)

✔ A plan for a few more adventures or troubles the character you introduced in Session 1 will get into—for example, Gretchen

✔ "How to Write Series Books" chart, prewritten (although you will make it seem like you create it together during the lesson) (see Teaching and Active Engagement)

✔ "Ways to Bring Stories to Life" chart from Unit 1, *Small Moments*, to use in a small group (see Conferring)

✔ "How to Write a Realistic Fiction Book" chart (see Share)

✔ A shared story in mind that you will develop with students. We use a class story about Charles who fell while skateboarding with his friend, Joe (see Share).

✔ A large five-page booklet (or chart paper to use as a booklet) to create the shared class story. The booklet or chart paper should have more lines on each page than children are used to seeing. (see Share)

COMMON CORE STATE STANDARDS: W.1.3, W.1.5, W.2.3, RL.1.1, RL.1.2, RL.1.3, RL.1.10, SL.1.1, SL.1.2, SL.1.4, L.1.1, L.1.2

IN THIS SESSION, you'll launch your writers into a new orbit. Yes, your six- and seven-year-olds will become the authors of series. Don't worry. This doesn't mean they have to create forty books in a series, as the author of the Magic Tree House did, or four thousand pages of text, as J. K. Rowling did. It means that once your students have invested some creative energy into a character, they can keep going with that character for a while, putting that character into new situations. When they tire of that character, they might create other characters who are in the same place or on the same team or in the same family. Or they may simply start a new series. Picture the boxed sets that students might make—and share that vision with your children. The very idea of a boxed set (perhaps a cereal box, painted, with a blurb about the famous young author on the back) is stirring for young writers. This is a new angle that will get them excited to write a lot, give them some new techniques to work on as writers, and shift their focus from coming up with new characters to doing more work with a few characters. It will also create clear moments of transference because students will have opportunities to pause, recall earlier strategies, and apply them with more independence. Remember, students read, or have been read, a lot of series. Young readers come of age on Poppleton, Henry and Mudge, Mr. Putter and Tabby, and Little Bill. They watch *Clifford* and *Sesame Street* and *SpongeBob* and *Star Wars*.

Henry and Mudge will thread through the rest of this unit as a familiar series. This session doesn't channel students to study those books as mentor texts deeply (though that will happen soon), but we do reference the series. So if you haven't done so yet, gather some books from this, or another beloved and familiar series, to have on hand and read often. If you're not sure about your students' experience with the series you select, and don't have time to share the series in class, you might send some copies home for bedtime reading, with a letter to parents, guardians, and siblings. Choose something you love, as you'll be reading and rereading this favorite often in the next few days.

You'll note in this lesson we encourage you to imagine what authors might have done as they created the series that students love. This is a favored method for writing teachers—taking beloved texts and imagining the work authors possibly did to make their books, so young writers can follow in their footsteps. Everything your children have learned so far about narrative writing will be useful to them. You'll want to give them opportunities to recall those skills, and then, as their excitement builds to become series writers, harness that excitement to stir them up to new endeavors.

"This session presents a new angle that will get students excited to write a lot, give them some new techniques to work on as writers, and shift their focus from coming up with new characters to doing more work with a few characters."

Series Writers Always Have a Lot to Write About

CONNECTION

Rally your children around how much they are growing as writers—create a little drama to stir up their fortitude before launching into the new work of series.

"Writers, you have already grown as fiction writers over the last week. I see you writing more than ever, and working more independently than ever. So before you learn a *new* thing today as fiction writers, can you think about what you are better at as a writer than you were just a few days ago? Not just what you're better at or what you've been working hard at from our checklist, but how you are working hard as an independent writer. Let's do it this way." I held up my hand, with my fingers bunched into a fist. "For each thing you are doing *even better* or *more independently*, unfold a finger, and wiggle it in the air." I demonstrated by holding up my fist, then unfolding my thumb and wiggling it back and forth. "Let's see how many fingers you can put up. Go ahead."

I watched as the children thought, and began to put fingers in the air. Soon some children had a whole hand raised. I interrupted them. "Now, quick, before you forget, turn and tell your partner what one of your fingers means—and when you say it, turn it down again so you'll know you explained it. Then explain another. Go ahead; tell each other about what you are doing even better and more independently."

As the children told each other what they were doing even better and more independently, I listened in. After a moment, I gathered the children back. "Writers!" I exclaimed. " I saw a lot of fingers in the air! Whole hands were wiggling! That means you are working hard to get stronger, every day. You are working at . . . " I wiggled my fingers in the air as I spoke, then turned them down for each quality I mentioned, "getting right to work, starting stories on your own . . . creating pretend characters . . . creating trouble and stretching that trouble down the page . . . fixing the trouble in your ending so that readers are satisfied . . . using everything you know to write more, like looking for paper with more lines . . . stapling in extra pages or booklets as you stretch your story out . . . writing *lots* of stories."

I put my fingers down. "What matters, writers, is that each of you is working hard at getting better as fiction writers. You haven't just nodded your head, and not really done anything new or hard. You've done the best possible work with your pretend characters. And today, because you've worked so hard, I think you are ready for something new. Today you are going to become series writers. And as series writers, I want to show you some new and exciting work you can do with your characters."

◆ COACHING

Returning to the theme of working hard, getting better, and being independent, makes it clear to students that the work of reflection is not the work of one lesson or one day, but is an ongoing habit for writers. This time, you can emphasize not just giving oneself directions, as you did earlier in the unit, but also that working hard and being independent are values in your writing workshop. Setting a strong work ethic will be as important as any individual strategy. A lot of what we do in writing workshop aims to stir children up to work hard at learning. Malcolm Gladwell, author of Outliers (2011), explains that the ability to work hard is one of the most crucial qualities of success—and thus it's one of the most important qualities to instill in your students.

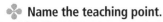 **Name the teaching point.**

"Writers, today I want to teach you that sometimes, when writers imagine a character they really like, they stick with that character for a bit and create more than one story around him or her. Fiction writers sometimes write series."

TEACHING

Return to a favorite series and notice what unites the stories.

"Writers, this work isn't that different from when you were writing lots of small moments. After all, those moments all had *you* as the most important character! And your house and your family and your pets were in a lot of those stories too. It's almost as if you were writing a series about yourself! And now you're writing a series of adventures about your new character. Think of the series you might want to write. Really picture it. Picture the boxed set, by you, the famous young author." I held up a boxed set. "For example, I'm writing the Gretchen series! This is probably how Harry Potter got started! J. K. Rowling wrote one story for Harry, and then she just wanted to keep giving him adventures.

"You can do this as well, writers. You can ask yourself, 'What do series writers do to come up with more than one story about a character that I could do too?' Let's think about that question. For instance, I'm thinking about some of the Henry and Mudge stories we've been reading." I held one up. "Now I'm asking myself, 'What did Cynthia Rylant do to come up with more than one story about these characters?' Let's see." I flipped through one of the copies of Henry and Mudge. "Well, with Henry and Mudge, I guess one obvious thing is that Henry and Mudge are in all the stories. So Cynthia Rylant decided to *keep going* with her characters." I picked up a second book and opened it, pausing at the table of contents. "But it's not the same *day* in each book. Each time, it's a new day. So Cynthia Rylant keeps having her characters start a new day in each story, or a new night."

I put down the book. "Writers, let's gather some of this thinking onto a chart. I'll start it now, and let's see what you can add to it." I flipped open the chart I'd started.

> ### How to Write Series Books
>
> - Use the same pretend characters.
> - Start a new day or night in each story.

John Hattie has written, in Visible Learning for Teachers *(2012), about the significance for learners of having a crystal clear goal they are trying to reach. Not only can this help writers follow a clear path, having a vision of the end product can stir them up to work harder. Play up the drama of their role as series authors and what their series might become, to role-play them into serious writers.*

ACTIVE ENGAGEMENT

Help your children articulate some of the work writers probably do as they create series around a character.

"Writers, right now, will you think of a series that you've read or watched on television that has the same character in it? If you can't think of one, there are some copies of Henry and Mudge, Little Bill, and some other series, right here in front of me. Give me a thumbs up when you've thought of a series that follows the same character." I waited a moment for the thumbs to go up. A few kids reached for a familiar series book. "Now, writers, think of a few episodes in this series, and think of our question: What do series writers do to come up with more than one story about a character? Turn and talk about what you notice about the series books we read. I'll listen in and try to gather what you're saying as you talk to your partner."

As they chatted about television shows and books, I gathered notes onto a chart, translating some language for them into "writerly language." I also quoted some of what they were saying aloud, to stir the pot.

"That's true, Avery, we do often get to know the character's family and friends, like Winnie the Pooh and Roo and Tigger, or Max and Ruby. And, yes, Nandika, sometimes we see the character in the same place a lot of the time. Oh, yes, Robin, right, the character is sort of the same in different stories."

Gather some of their thinking onto the chart. Later, you might put some pictures of familiar characters next to the words, to make this thinking more memorable.

I motioned for their attention. "Writers, I've gathered some of your thinking onto this chart."

- Have things happen in the same place.
- Include the same friend, pet, brother, or sister.
- Write different adventures.

"Wow, writers, this is great thinking. I can tell you've read a lot of Mr. Putter and Tabby, and Star Wars, and Winnie the Pooh! This is going to be so much fun, writing series books. You can do the work these authors did, and maybe your series will be a famous boxed set, like the Magic Tree House collection, or Harry Potter!" Their faces lit up as they thought about all their stories making a famous collection.

HOW TO WRITE
SERIES BOOK!

- Use the same pretend characters
- Start a new day or night in each story
- Have things happen in the same place
- Include the same friend, pet, brother, sister
- Write different adventures

Pinky + Rex Clifford Spiderman
Henry + Mudge Mr. Putter + Tabby

LINK

Recall with your students what they've been learning, and help them give themselves orders for how they might spend their time as writers.

"Before you leave the meeting area, will you make a quick plan as a writer—will you give yourself orders about what you are going to do? Here are some choices." I put up a finger for each. "One, you keep going with a character you've been writing about. That means you're ready to go write. Two, you want to create a new pretend character for your series and you're ready to start that now. Three, you want to start a new character and series, but you need to finish the story you're writing now first.

"You know how to give yourselves directions, writers. What are you going to *do* as a writer today?" I held up each finger and whispered the options again, motioning for them to start giving themselves orders. I tapped their shoulders as they finished to send them off to work.

Once again, your link is your opportunity to review prior instruction and emphasize the repertoire that children are developing. Naming the choices they might make helps them be independent.

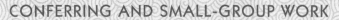

Elaborating by Bringing Stories to Life

TODAY YOU HAVE EMPHASIZED the importance of students carrying forward what they've learned and working hard and with independence. There is one aspect that can be challenging with this emphasis on agency and transference—and that is carrying strategies forward over time, not just over a day or two. It's a little bit like reading a longer book, and needing to remember what happened at the beginning, much later. You want your writers to reach back, and put into play all that you taught them months ago during your last narrative unit of study.

Some writers will do this automatically. They either remember the actual strategies you taught, and even use the academic jargon you used (perhaps you've heard a child say "I'm planning my writing"), or they remember the gist of the work they did, and they simply keep doing it. These writers don't really need you to get out old charts, or prior writing, to remind them of what they learned months ago. Other children do. Some especially need support carrying forward the narrative craft moves—the stuff that makes their storytelling better.

MID-WORKSHOP TEACHING   **Series Writers Sometimes Have Characters Get into Predictable Trouble**

"Writers, I want to tell you something that I noticed from the series books we've been reading. Often the authors have characters get into similar trouble. Like in the Harry the Dirty Dog series, for example, Harry is always getting into similar scrapes! That got me thinking that I could also have my character get into similar trouble.

"In one of my Gretchen stories that I've been writing, Gretchen gets into trouble because she didn't listen to her mother. And now I'm thinking that in a new story, I could have Gretchen get into trouble again because she didn't listen. Wouldn't that be cool? That way, Gretchen has predictable trouble across several stories!

"But I want to tell you something else, writers. Even though I'm going to have Gretchen get into similar trouble, writers also think about different ways to get their character out of trouble. That's what makes series books so fun, isn't it? We never know how the character is going to get out of trouble *this* time! So for my story, I'm going to have Gretchen get out of trouble the first time by apologizing, but in the next story, I think I'm going to have Gretchen get out of trouble by remembering at the last minute what her mother told her.

"Writers, see if this would work for you. Turn and tell your partner if you have any ideas for trouble your character might get into that could be the same across stories, and different ways for getting your character *out* of trouble. As you talk, I'm going to add this strategy to our chart. And if you have other ideas as series writers, you know you can always share those too."

How to Write Series Books

- Use the same pretend characters.
- Start a new day or night in each story.
- Have things happen in the same place
- Include the same friend, pet, brother, or sister.
- Write different adventures.
- Have trouble repeat sometimes.

To help children recall what they learned about improving their narratives, you could lean on a few tools. You might have students work closely with the Narrative Writing Checklists again in this session. Or, you might bring forth students' prior narrative writing—their on-demand pieces, or their published pieces from your first narrative unit. Or, you might bring out a chart that students used in a prior unit, and perhaps the demonstration text that you wrote during your earlier unit. Whichever tool you use to scaffold children's recall, your goal is to increase transference, and the chart, demo text, or on-demand piece is a physical artifact to stimulate children's recall.

For example, you'll undoubtedly see the need to reteach some elaboration strategies. In your first unit of study, on small moments, those included bringing their stories to life by making characters move and speak, telling their stories bit by bit, and developing the inner feelings of characters. You touched on some of these strategies in Session 3, but some students may need more than just a reminder to bring forth all that they've learned. To recall this important work, it might go like this. Look across your children's writing. First, give table conferences to writers who *are* transferring prior instruction. "Anika," you might say, "I love the way you are bringing out characters' inner feelings in your story, just like you did in your small moment writing—in the pictures and the words. I can really tell how afraid your character is when you write she was shaking in fear!" Soon other writers as that table will be adding in words for feelings. It's always worth it to try a few table conferences first, because some writers will simply hear what you compliment, and begin to do more of that. Then you can concentrate on the ones who need more pointed explanations and examples.

I found myself pulling one such small group, and decided to work with the children on some of the elaboration work they had done during the *Small Moments* unit. First, you might think about what scaffold to use. I pulled in this familiar chart.

Ways to Bring Stories to Life

- "Unfreeze" people—make them move, make them talk
- Tell small steps
- Bring out the inside—make people feel, make people think

Then you can have the kids set goals and reflect on what they have done well so far and what they plan to do more of.

For this small group, I said, "Writers, does this chart look familiar?" as I pointed to the chart. "Remember we used this in small moments and then brought it out again in one of our minilessons in this unit? Well, I was thinking it could really help you as you write your series books. You could reread the story you are working on now then look at the list and name what you are already doing. Then you could ask yourself, 'What else can I be doing?' Finally, make a plan and a commitment of what you can do more of.

"So, right now, read your fiction book." I waited a minute while the children read their own pieces and then asked, "Okay, what have you been doing already, and what can you do more of?" As they did this, I gestured dramatically, pointing to the chart. I whispered, "Alejandra, did you write what your character said?"

Alejandra said, "I already made my character move bit by bit, but I didn't make my character talk very much. I could do more of that." Miles said, "Me too! I need to do that some more too!"

I then asked the kids to point to the place in their books where they could do it right now. We repeated this exercise once more, reading their work, pointing to the chart and then their own writing, and they got to work, with the goal of writing more and remembering things they have done before. I told them I would check in on them at the end of writing time to see how they were doing and reminded them that they could do this from now on in all their fiction books.

When I returned to this small group to see if they added a bit more elaboration in their writing, Alejandra had added in speech bubbles to her sketch, and some dialogue to her text. Miles, though, was continuing to write without elaboration. I pulled out another tool—the demonstration texts I had from our first unit and this unit. Pulling those out, I showed Miles how I had brought characters to life in the Small Moment story about the fire drill that I had used in class during our first narrative unit. I pointed to the line, "Quick, everyone, line up!" Miles laughed as he remembered this story. Then I pointed to the line "Peep, peep, CAW!" in my more recent fiction story about Gretchen. Looking at these examples of characters talking, Miles began to nod. "Do it just like that, Miles," I said. "Give yourself directions to add one bit of dialogue on this page, and see how that brings your characters to life." Next time I looked over, Miles was adding bits of dialogue, and looking closely from the demonstration texts, back to his own writing.

Shared Writing

Recruit the class to help co-construct a shared plan for what will become a class story. Channel students to coauthor the idea of the main character and possible ideas for the trouble the character will get into, tucking in tips for how to stretch out a realistic fiction book.

"Writers, you are all doing so well on your series books! You know how we often write pieces together so we can practice tricky stuff? Well, I want to show you how to stretch out realistic fiction stories by using what we know about writing small moments to help us. You can stretch each *part* of your story like it is a small moment. You can stretch out the 'getting into trouble part' of the story *and* the 'fixing and solving the trouble part.' This will be exciting, and it seems like the perfect time for us to make up a class character and write a fiction book together too!" Of course, that brought on a big burst of "Yeah!"

"Okay, so let's look back at our chart of how to write a realistic fiction book so we remember what to do to get started." I gestured to each item on the chart. "So, we need to think of a pretend character and give him or her a name and some places where he might go." I tapped my head to gesture that it was time to think and paused to give them a little thinking time. "Turn and talk to your partner about your ideas."

After quick negotiations we settled on the name Charles, and a little more chatter produced some ideas about Charles, including that he would be a seven-year-old boy who loves riding his skateboard in front of his house, drinking soda, and playing at his friend Joe's house.

"Now, let's imagine some possible trouble that Charles can get into. Thumbs up if you have some ideas. Remember, it is helpful to begin by thinking about where Charles will be. Where can the story take place? What will happen to Charles? Let's focus on the trouble part of the story!" I called on kids to get some possibilities.

Some ideas from kids were Charles really, really wants a new, fancy skateboard but can't afford it. Charles leaves his block without permission and gets lost. Charles did something bad and then felt awful. Out of all the suggestions, we decided on Charles falling off his skateboard because he was showing off to Joe, drinking soda at the same time, and badly hurting himself.

After selecting a story focus for the class based on the suggestions shared, I pointed to a five-page booklet on chart paper and said, "We are ready to tell the first part of our story—the trouble Charles gets into—across a few of these

When you're coauthoring with students, it's helpful to think about stories that will really engage your students—which means tackling issues or problems they know something about and can write well. Making your main character their age, and giving him or her a kind of "coolness" (such as being a skateboarder), makes the character fascinating to kids. Showing the character's flaws makes him real.

pages. Do you see how there are more lines now on these pages? That's because we are going to stretch out and say more about the first part of the story, using what we know about small moments.

"So, let's plan. The first page can be about skateboarding with Joe, the second page can be showing off and the third page can be about falling down. Now, let's try to stretch each page and show the trouble moment with lots of detail! Right now, with your partner, tell how this first page could go. Remember, it needs to sound like the books we read, with lots of details. We know Charles is showing off and will fall. So, what exactly was Charles doing? How did he feel? What did he say? Remember, you can bring your stories to life! Use your fingers to tell the first part of the story!"

After listening in, I gathered the class back together and said, "Wow! You all have such great ideas for the beginning of this story. Listen to me retell it. Move your fingers each time you hear details to stretch down the page. See if we are really using everything we know about small moments on each page." In my best storyteller voice, I told the beginning of the story using words, phrases, and ideas I heard from the kids. As I told it, I wrote the details on the first page of the big chart paper booklet.

> Page 1: One morning, Charles was skateboarding with his friend Joe. "Look how fast I am going," said Charles. "I can catch you," Joe replied.

"Did you all use lots of details?" The students nodded. "I thought you did too. You really stretched the details *down* the page. Let's do the same with the next two pages of the trouble moment!"

I gave kids time on the next two pages to stretch out the trouble part with details. And then I recorded what they said:

> Page 2: They were chasing each other and showing off. "Look at me," Charles said drinking his soda. He didn't see the big rock on the sidewalk. "Watch out!" screamed Joe.

> Page 3: Charles tumbled over the rock. The soda can went flying. He fell. His knee was gushing with blood.

Channel students to coauthor possible ideas for how the character will get out of trouble, again tucking in tips for how to stretch out a realistic fiction book.

"Wow, these pages really tell about the trouble part so far, writers," I said, touching the pages again and retelling. "See how we have three whole pages and how we stretched our small moment down the page! Some of you might have noticed that we used lots of details, four or five details on some of the pages. Now, let's imagine the ending and how the characters are going to get out of trouble! What did Charles do? What did Joe do? How would you stretch that part of the story across pages? Turn and talk with your partner, and I'll listen in."

Again, I listened in and then gathered the class back. "These are some great ideas for the second half of our story—the fixing and solving the trouble that the characters are in. So, on this page," I touched the fourth page of our booklet, "we can write about how Joe goes to get help for Charles. And on this page," I touched the fifth page of the booklet, "we

Capture your shared writing so that students (and you) can refer to it again and again, pointing to parts that you can use as examples.

can write how Joe and Charles's dad help Charles walk home. Those were some great ideas I heard. Let's try and use all that we know about writing with detail to help stretch this part of the story down the page! Are you ready to try? Let's do page 4. Joe going to find help! Turn and talk."

After several moments, I called students back. "Listen to what I heard. Count the details." I began to say back what one partnership said.

Page 4: Joe ran all the way back to Charles's house.

"Should we add another detail to stretch this part of the story down the page? What could we add? Turn and talk."

I gave the kids a second opportunity to stretch down the page using what they know about adding details. "Here are two more details, listen. 'He looked for Charles's dad. Joe said, "Help! Help! Charles is bleeding."' I am going to record that part here, while you all turn and talk about page 5, where they help Charles. Turn and talk!"

I wrote the page as fast as I could and then listened into their ideas. I voiced over to the group to think about another detail and to try to fill up their hands and the page with details about the part.

"Listen up! Annabel has a great way to start this page."

Annabel said, "Joe and Charles's dad ran down the street with towels and bandaids. The dad said, 'It's okay Charles.' Dad helped Charles. Joe got the skateboard. Then they walked home."

"Thank you Annabel! Anything we should make Charles say or feel at the end?"

"I think Charles should say, 'I'll never do that again!'" Miles chimed in.

"I agree. I love it. I'll write that part in later. I love how this story has two parts—the getting into trouble part and the fixing and solving part!"

I motioned to the children's folders. "Writers, before we stop, I know that you are thinking about your stories and some of you may be thinking, 'Wait! I need to stretch out details down my pages too!' Or you may be thinking, 'I need more pages!' No worries. We will have writing workshop tomorrow and you will have a chance to go back to your stories and stretch them out by writing details down the page!"

When you coauthor a piece with your children, your "questions" can also act as prompts, leading your students through the steps of writing small moments with detail, action, and dialogue.

You don't have to actually record the entire piece in front of the children. The goal is to help them practice elaboration. They may suggest some of these details, and you'll take the time later to record them.

Introducing Your Character in Book One of a Series

What Does Your Reader Want to Know?

B Y NOW MANY OF YOUR WRITERS will feel as if they are up to their elbows in the work of being a series author—and yet your job will be to teach them today how to write Book One in their series. You might think, "*Book One*? The kids are already primed to write Book Three." We grasp that, but here's our point: to really write Book One well requires an author to have a plan for the overall series—something your writers will only begin to grasp now—and it requires also a better understanding of how series books go. Now that your series writers know more, it is a good time to go back and revise. This will hopefully help them plan for future books.

You've launched this work, setting your students up to think about what series writers do that they could do as well, and this work will continue to thread across the unit. As you scaffold your students' revision work, another way to forge connections across reading and writing is to consider the levels of the stories your children are reading, and plan some writing work around stories at that level.

If you have read a lot of series books with children, and if you have studied what makes these stories more challenging as readers move up levels of text complexity, you may have noticed that not all series are the same. At the Reading and Writing Project, we have studied bands of text complexity, and we've written about this work in our reading units of study. One way series become more complicated as you move from the G-H-I-J band of text complexity to the K-L-M band is that the order in which you read them begins to matter more. Think of the Magic Treehouse series. Can you read them out of order? Yes, of course. But does the series make even more sense if you begin with Book One? Yes. In Book One, the details of Jack and Annie's relationship are laid out. How the tree house works is explained. Each later book builds on details that were presented in Book One. Series books in G-H-I-J do this as well, of course, but the stories build on each other less. Book One of Henry and Mudge (which is actually called *The First Book*) gives details on where Henry lives, how lonely it is there, and how and why Henry gets his big dog, Mudge. Book One of Mr. Putter and Tabby gives details on how sad Mr. Putter was before Tabby, where Tabby comes from, and on the beginning of their relationship.

IN THIS SESSION, you'll teach children that series writers often write a Book One to their series. In it, they share a lot of details about their character.

GETTING READY

✔ Two excerpts (that you'll have written in booklets ahead of time) of different stories about the character which you've been modeling, for example, Gretchen (see Connection)

✔ A collection of series books, such as Henry and Mudge, Mr. Putter and Tabby, and Poppleton, that have a Book One that introduces the characters in some detail (see Teaching)

✔ Sample excerpts from the stories you used in your Connection that demonstrate how authors tuck details into story structure (see Conferring)

✔ A revision basket, including revision strips, extra pages, tape, staplers, booklets (see Conferring)

COMMON CORE STATE STANDARDS: W.1.3, W.1.5, W.1.8, W.2.3, RL.1.1, RL.1.2, RL.1.3, RL.1.10, SL.1.1, SL.1.5, L.1.1, L.1.2.a

You might, then, think about where the majority of your writers are as readers when you think about scaffolding their work for writing Book One in their series. If many of them have read or are reading G-H-I-J, as we suspect, then you may lead children to mimic the work that Book One does in the kinds of series they are reading. You may also have some readers who are familiar with Magic Treehouse–type series (level M). They might then use these as a model. Children will benefit from looking closely at the first books in any of the familiar series they are reading, and moving to accomplish some of that same work in their own writing. Having students study how authors introduce characters in the books they are reading will also help you link the close reading work advocated by the Common Core Standards and the narrative elaboration you're striving for.

The challenge of the work today will be that students not only introduce their characters in an all-about fashion, but that they do so within a narrative structure. This may take some practice for some of your writers, because they may at first want to list the characteristics of their characters, rather than allowing the details to come through in a Small Moment story. With some scaffolding, though, and work with mentor texts, your writers will take to this and soon be off writing up a storm, tucking details about their character into a small moment, working in a new book or adding on to books they've already started.

Really, of course, this is a lesson on writing more, on elaboration, and on thinking like a writer with a real audience. The kids, though, will think it is putting them on the road toward becoming Cynthia Rylant, which is all to the good.

"Having students study how authors introduce characters in the books they are reading will also help you link the close reading work advocated by the Common Core Standards and the narrative elaboration you're striving for."

Introducing Your Character in Book One of a Series

What Does Your Reader Want to Know?

CONNECTION

Invite children to decide if the book you are writing sounds as if it could be the first book in a series, or if it sounds like a later story.

"Writers, gather around. I'm going to read you some of my Gretchen books. I've been thinking about what order I might put my books in, and also if I need to do any extra work in the first book in my series. So can you help me? If the book I read sounds like it is Book One—if it just seems like it would come first—will you give this signal?" I made a signal with two arms in the air, as if I were starting a Nascar race. "If it sounds like something else—a story that comes later in the series, when the reader *already* knows the characters, will you do this?" I put both arms crossed in front of me. "Got the signals? Do them with me. Arms in the air for sounds like Book One, arms crossed for doesn't." I flourished my booklets. Then I read:

Introducing playful elements such as waving your arms in the air helps your serious writing workshop feel joyful (and developmentally appropriate). So does the noisy drama of the story. "Peep, peep, CAW!" should ring through your classroom, startling children out of complacency!

> Gretchen heard a noise. "Peep, peep, CAW! Peep, peep, CAW!" "What is that?" she thought. She crouched down on the path. It was a fierce bird. Gretchen felt afraid. "I'll be brave," she thought. She scooped up the bird in her sweater.

"What do you think?" Arms were mostly crossed. "I agree. This sounds like you already know who Gretchen is, and about her fort. Not like the first book in the series. Here's another."

> Gretchen had just moved to the country. One day she was in the forest by her new house. "I wish I could have a tree fort," Gretchen thought. Sometimes Gretchen was lonely. She wanted a place to play. She looked around the woods. She wondered, "What could I build a fort with?"

Arms were in the air. "Aha! I bet I could turn this into Book One! It sounds like the first time we're meeting Gretchen."

Explain that the first book in a series and later books in the same series might sound different, without explaining in detail why that is.

I motioned for children to put their arms down. "Writers, what you just heard was the difference between a story that starts right in the middle of the action, and a story that gives some details about who and where the character is. Both

You'll notice that we explain after demonstrating. Explanations are more meaningful when children attach them to an example.

are good ways to start a story. But the second is more like a first story. The very first book in a *series* plays a special role—it introduces the character and the character's world—so that readers will be set up for all the other books that follow."

❖ Name the teaching point.

"Writers, today I want to teach you that series writers often tell a lot of important details about their characters in *Book One* of their series. This helps the reader understand the characters better and know what to look for in other books in the series. "

TEACHING

Recall with students that many of the mentor texts they have been reading have a Book One that introduces the characters to the reader.

"I began to wonder about the first book in a series when yesterday Annabelle asked me, 'When does Henry get his big dog, Mudge?' Last night, I reread the very first Henry and Mudge book that Cynthia Rylant wrote—in fact, it's called *The First Book*—to see if I could answer the question. And guess what? The answer was in that first book! Then I started thinking about other series we've been reading in the same way. I asked myself, 'When did Mr. Putter get Tabby? How did Poppleton meet Cherry Sue?' and 'Do all these series have a first book that tells the reader special stuff?' As I asked these questions, I revealed the first book of each of these series.

Demonstrate investigating what authors often do in the first book of a series.

"Writers, I discovered that there is a lot of information that goes into a first book of a series—it's as if the author is saying, 'Reader, here are the things you need to know about this character.' So let's look at a few of these Book Ones together, and notice what kind of stuff an author puts into a Book One. Here's Book One of Henry and Mudge." I flipped through the pages and said, "Hmmm . . . Cynthia Rylant tells us that Henry is an only child, that he is lonely. That he could use a best friend. Then she tells about how Henry gets Mudge. There's the answer to Annabelle's question!

"So Cynthia Rylant gives us lots of details about the character, Henry, in this first book. Let's look at these other two books and see if we can name the *kinds* of details the author puts into a first book."

I picked up a second book and said, "Book One, Mr. Putter and Tabby. Let's see . . . Cynthia Rylant tells us that Mr. Putter lives alone. She tells us that Mr. Putter likes English muffins, and tea, and stories.

"So what kinds of details are these? Hmmm . . . They seem to be details about who the character is, where the character lives, and what he likes. I'm going to keep a list of these for now, so we can keep track of things that go into Book One of a series."

On chart paper, I jotted:

We refer to several Cynthia Rylant series here because we love them, and because the children know them from prior grades and reading workshop. You'll want to refer to characters that are familiar to your students. Feel free to include references and characters from comic books and television series to make your point. Every series has an origin story.

Details that Go in Book One of a Series
✓ Who the character is
✓ Where character lives
✓ What character likes

"What else? Well, the author tells us that Mr. Putter has no one to tell his stories to. Then there are details about how he got Tabby . . . " I let my voice trail off. Then I said, "Wait a minute! That's just like what Cynthia Rylant did in Henry and Mudge. In both books, the author tells us that the character is a little lonely. She tells us how the characters *feel*." I added that to the list. "And then she introduces us to characters that are important to the main character—to Mudge and to Tabby."

✓ How the character feels
✓ Who the character's best friends are

ACTIVE ENGAGEMENT

Set students up for a mini-inquiry. Give them a Book One from a different series and add any new observations they come up with to the growing list.

I picked up a third book. "I'm going to retell a little of Book One, Poppleton. As I do, would you be ready to turn and talk to your partner about what you notice? You can look up at the list I made, to see if those kinds of details are in *this* Book One, too.

"Let's see. Cynthia Rylant describes Poppleton before he moved to the country. She says that he took taxis, jogged in the park, went to museums. Then she tells us why he moved to the country, and there are details about how he met Cherry Sue. Hmm . . . I think we're beginning to see a pattern here. Quick, turn and tell your partner what you noticed the author doing in this Book One."

As children turned and talked, I listened in and overheard Nora say to her partner, "She tells you how the characters began." I added in, "Yes, that's interesting. Not really how they began as a baby, but how they began a friendship, or began to live someplace, or do something. That's the case with the first two books, too, isn't it? We hear about Henry before he got Mudge, and about Mr. Putter before he got Tabby. Nice detecting, Nora!"

Debrief, summarizing the work children did and setting them up to follow similar steps in their own stories.

"Writers, I heard lots of you say that Cynthia Rylant also tells us about what Poppleton likes—in this case, what he likes to do. And you also noticed that she introduces a character who will be important to the main character throughout the series—Cherry Sue. Nora noticed that Cynthia Rylant also talks about how characters come to be in a place or how they become friends with other characters.

Book One of A Series Has
▭ Who the character is
▭ Where the character lives
▭ What the character likes
▭ How the character feels
▭ Who the character's best friends are
▭ Important background information!

It might be helpful to read aloud a book you have already read aloud in reading workshop. Choose a familiar favorite.

"I'm going to add what we noticed to our list."

Details that Go in Book One of a Series

✓ Who the character is
✓ Where the character lives
✓ What the character likes
✓ How the character feels
✓ Who the character's best friends are
✓ How the character comes to be in a place
✓ How the character becomes friends with other characters

Channel children's energy into introducing their characters.

"Writers, what you just noticed these mentor authors doing, you can do that work for your character too! You can introduce your character by giving details about the things your character likes, where your character lives, the special place your character is, or special friends." As I spoke I pointed to the kinds of details we had listed.

"Writers, let's give you a chance to practice introducing your characters. Right now, imagine that your partner doesn't know your character." I waited a moment. "What *kinds* of details do you want to share about your character? Does your character have a special place you could describe? Does your character have a special friend? Quick, turn and introduce your character to your partner. Remember to use lots of important details. Use our list if you need help!"

I listened in and then voiced over, "Writers, listen to Robert's introduction." I nudged Robert to begin.

My character is Benjamin. He used to live in Canada, but he came here this year. On the first day of school, he was so nervous! He told his mom, "I don't want to go!" He walked slow, slow, slow, on the way to school.

"Robert did something we might all copy. He gave us details in his introduction *and* he made it interesting by making it sound like a story. He said, 'On the first day of school . . . ,' and then he began one small moment."

As they continued, I added in some commentary so children could hear more storytelling language. "Joshua, I like how you said, 'Before Jack and Sam became friends Jack didn't know anyone in the park. Then one day, he was in the sandbox, and there was a boy with a truck.' Those are important details, and you made me interested in your story, too." Once introductions were made, I gathered the students back together.

In a minilesson, you use every literary device possible to create a text—a minilesson—that is compelling enough that it will merit the attention of six-year-olds! Here, you'll notice we use repetition and exaggeration around "Book One" to draw children in and to highlight the important point. It's important that you not elaborate about any one of the books. The whole point is that this is a list, one that shows that in series after series, the first book accomplishes the same job.

You always want clear signals in your room for gathering and releasing attention. Some teachers rely on bells or turning the lights on and off. Peter Johnston sometimes speaks about teaching children to take up behaviors you want them to show as adults. So you might also consider nonverbal signals, or quiet hand motions, the kind of methods you might use to gather respectful adults back together in a meeting.

What Robert did naturally was to give his details within a small moment. Helping children begin with "The moment when . . . " or "One day . . . " will help cue up their storytelling voice. Often, when you really listen in on what children do during active engagement, you'll find a few students whom you can use as models. You can prop them up by rehearsing with them, to get the most out of every precious instructional moment.

LINK

Invite writers to plan their writing work for the day, reminding them of all the choices they have.

"Writers, before you dive into writing, you know how important it is to plan your work. Take one second and think about your plan for today. Some of you are working on a book from yesterday. Do you want to tape in a page or two at the beginning of that book, to introduce your character? Some of you are ready to start a new book. Do you want to write a new book that will be Book One in your series? Or maybe you have other important work to finish. Quick, turn and tell your partner. What will you work on today?"

As children finished their plans, I tapped them on the shoulder to send them each off to write. As I did so, I listened not just for what they wanted to say, but if they had a plan for what they would do today.

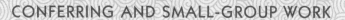
Studying How Authors Tuck Details into Stories

WHEN YOU INVITE YOUNG WRITERS to add lots of details about characters, you invite them into work that delights and challenges writers of any age. It's enormous fun to *imagine* details about a character—to imagine the character's family and home, what the character likes to do, even his or her clothes. If you look carefully at some of the sketches in your children's stories, you'll notice that some of these are amazingly consistent in the details of the house the character lives in, or the striped shirt the character wears in different scenes. These children picture the details of their imaginary character's life in their mind, and tuck those details into little spots of their stories.

The challenge of this work is that it can sometimes turn into a lot of lists that are only details, or isolated details about a character, and there's no action, no *story* for awhile! "Rosie loved chocolate milk. She drank it every day. She also loved her cat, Suzie. Suzie was her best friend." You may want to ask yourself—do you care if children end up with some pages that are lists, or some details that don't really add much to the story's problem or tension? After all, any elaboration, anything that gets them to write with more detail, more description, and more words, is a good thing.

In this case, the work of tucking introductory details into storytelling structure wasn't work I wanted to worry about with most of my writers. But I did have in mind a group of strong writers (who were also strong readers) who I thought would be interested in this challenge. I pulled these writers together, and said, "Writers, I've been thinking about you as writers. I expected that it wouldn't be that hard for you to come up with details to introduce your character. Am I right, that was easy for you?" Nods, smiles. The phrase, "I've been thinking about you as writers," is a powerful one for a teacher. Annabel opened her booklet to show us some of her details.

"I think you're ready, then, to study a tricky part of this work. If it's easy for you to come up with details, you're ready to study how writers tuck these details into the *action* of their story."

There are different ways that writers tuck in introductory details, from putting them in the pictures or inner thinking (Henry pictures himself playing baseball with another boy), to putting them in dialogue ("I want a brother," he told his parents), to putting them into action. I decided to introduce action because it seemed within easy reach of these writers, and the mentor texts they were familiar with did this work repeatedly.

MID-WORKSHOP TEACHING
Writers Fix Up Their Writing as They Go, Including Capitals

"Writers, can I pause you for one moment? I've seen so many of you adding details about your characters, about their best friends, their animals, their favorite things to do, or their favorite places to go. You're all doing such amazing work. I want to remind you that when writers revise and add more to their writing, they don't forget all the things they know to do to make their writing easy to read. Instead, they make sure to check their writing for capitals and punctuation. Most of you are using capitals to start a sentence, but are you also using capital letters for your characters' names? Right now, look at your writing and check to see if you are using capital letters for all your characters and at the start of sentences. Go back and fix up any missing capitals if you see some are missing!

"I bet you all have ideas for other things you could fix up in your writing, too. Capital letters might just be one of these things. Writers fix things up all the time as they are writing."

I opened up a story I had brought with me. "Listen to this, writers. I'm going to read you just a few lines from Book One of Henry and Mudge. Listen for how Cynthia Rylant tucks details about the character into a *list of actions*. This is when Henry's parents are deciding whether Henry should be allowed to get a dog." I read aloud, "'First they looked at their house with no brothers or sisters. Then they looked at their street with no children. Then they looked at Henry's face.' Did you hear it, the list of actions? Say it back, that will help you really hear it." The children nodded, saying back, "looked at the house, looked at the street, looked at Henry."

I picked up another book. "Now listen to this, from *Poppleton*. Actually, it's kind of interesting how these first books have titles that are just the names of the characters. I wonder if that's a sign that it's Book One." I saw them tuck that idea away for their own series. I fully expected that soon, many students would be titling their first books in their series this way. "Ready? Are you listening for how the author tucks in a list of actions?" I flipped to page 1 and read how Poppleton took taxis, jogged in the park, and went to museums.

At hand were staplers, tape, paper, revision strips, and extra pages. "Are you ready, writers? Do you want to try adding in details about your character in a list of actions?" Nods. "If you do this work, maybe you can show it to some other writers, and teach them, using your piece as well as Cynthia Rylant's books?" Stronger nods. Asking children to propagate your teaching by doing the work in their own writing, even if they end up not being able to explain it all that well to another writer, often stirs them up to really focus and work hard, and it calls on community values of sharing and helping.

The children got to work. Soon I looked over Annabel's story and saw that where the first page of her story had been "Mary's class went to the see the sea animals," now it started, "One day, Mary was going to a big aquarium. Mary was on a field trip. She was on the bus. Mary was excited. Mary was finding a seat." Annabel was mentoring herself to Cynthia Rylant.

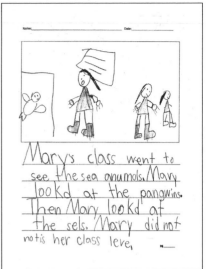

FIG. 7–1   In this part of her story, Annabel tries out the technique of listing actions as a way to tuck in details about a new character.

Pretending to Be Our Characters

Invite your writers to do pretend interviews with their characters, encouraging them to ask and answer questions in dramatic role-play, and to make stuff up!

"A famous author once said that fiction writers need to know their characters *so well* that they know how much change the characters carry in their pockets. I don't think that famous author really cares about whether the character has two quarters or three in his pocket, but the point is we need to know our characters' stories and personalities and families and worries really well. And that means we need to make up a lot of stuff about our characters. I thought we could help each other make up more details about our characters if we pretended our characters were right next to us, sitting right here"—I drew forth an empty chair—"and we asked our character some questions.

"Let's say that Oscar the Grouch was sitting in this chair. Think of the questions you'd want to ask him." I gave a moment of silence. "Might you ask, 'Why do you live in a garbage can, Oscar?' Or, 'How do you like Sesame Street?' Well, we could go on, but what I'd love to have you do is to interview *your* character right now. Pick up an imaginary phone and call your character. As the phone rings, think about what you want to ask your character." I left a few seconds for phones to ring and characters to answer. "Now, in your mind, ask your character a question or two—a question that goes with your stories." I gave a moment of silence. "Now here's the hard part—try to answer that question as your character. To do that you will need to *make stuff up*. You'll need to invent stuff. Imagine in your head, and answer as your character. Whisper what you'd say.

"Now, turn to your partner, and *be your character*. Talk about yourself, answering the questions you asked. Partner 1, you start. After you've answered your questions, listen to Partner 2 be his or her character. You might even repeat the question first so your answers make sense. Like, 'Why do I live in a garbage can? Well, that's because I love trash!'"

The children began to role-play, naturally expanding this drama. Some of them decided to call their character back, to answer more questions. Some characters began to interview each other. Some began to answer a question by telling part of a story. Amos, in character, said, "What do I most love to do? I love movies and baseball. In my first story, I watch a movie about baseball!" Later I heard, "What do I have in my pocket? Not quarters. I have baseball cards."

"Writers, whenever you are writing fiction, remember that it's also pretend! You can play with making stuff up—you can interview your character, draw your character, dress your character, imagine what's in your character's pockets!"

Writers Develop Their Dialogue

Dear Teachers,

If you have been following the order suggested for first-grade units, many months ago your children used their hands as puppets to rehearse what they might say in their Small Moment stories. In this session, you might decide to return to the skill of bringing stories to life with dialogue. If you decide to use our template here to design your own minilesson, you'll harness some of children's skills at pretending and at role-playing, and you'll teach them new strategies that writers use to develop dialogue. We hope this letter inspires you to capitalize on all you have taught, holding kids accountable for what they have learned and, at the same time, teaching them to build on those skills, transferring what they've learned earlier in the year to a new type of writing.

MINILESSON

In your connection part of today's minilesson you might invite your children to share some of the things that they've said, or that people have said to them, since they woke up that day. Invite them to include any "speaking sharply," any dramatic moments, the dialogue that they remember best. As they share with a partner, listen in and capture some of what they say on chart paper, listing, for example, "When people speak, they . . . yell, cry, shout, whisper." You might finish your connection by thinking about which of these things the characters in your stories might do when they talk.

Next, your teaching point might be that writers make characters in their stories speak in many ways, just as people in real life do. You might decide which specific moves your writers might be ready for next, based on what they are doing now with their dialogue. Following are a few possibilities that might be helpful, based on what the needs of your writers might be. Keep in mind that you can also do some of these in one-on-one conferences or small groups.

COMMON CORE STATE STANDARDS: W.1.3, W.1.5, W.2.3, RL.1.1, RL.1.3, RL.1.4, RFS.1.1, RFS.1.4, SL.1.1, SL.1.4, SL.1.6, L.1.1, L.1.2

If . . .	Then . . .
• You see characters talking only in speech bubbles	• Model how writers add sentences on the lines under the picture box of what the character said
• You see characters saying something but no one is talking back	• Model one character saying something to another, having a conversation
• You see kids using dialogue with only the word *said*	• Teach other tags they could use to describe how characters may have sounded, for example, *shouted*, *cried*, or *whispered*
• You see speech bubbles and thought bubbles	• Show writers how to add "she said" and "she thought" to their writing underneath the picture
• You see exciting dialogue that adds to the action of the story	• Show writers how to add body movements, for example, "She put up her hands and yelled, 'KEEP BACK!'"

To demonstrate these techniques, you might return to the story you started as a shared writing piece, about Charles and Joe—or the characters you made up—and do some role-playing of what one character might say and do. Remember that when you model, you can show the kids that they can do this type of work in more than one place in their story. Sometimes you may see evidence of kids doing something, but they only do it once. They'll need reminders to transfer what they've learned to other parts of their writing, and in other books on other days. This will set you up well to demonstrate developing your dialogue in one part of the story, and for children to practice adding dialogue in a second part.

During the active engagement you can have kids return to the shared writing you've done, and role-play more of what Charles and Joe might have said when Charles falls down. You might have them act out parts of the story in partnerships, adding in the body movements, what characters say, and what they say back to each other. You may decide to have the kids practice the dialogue work you just demonstrated and also add in some work on making characters move.

Offering choice is an important teaching move to strengthen independence. You can reference the work they did when you studied the craft moves of George McClements in *Night of the Veggie Monster*. Remind the class that George was telling the exact actions of what the character did: curling his toes and wiggling his fingers. You may say to kids, "Let's make the characters do something *and* say something. Instead of just saying it fast, we can say it longer and fill up pages with action and dialogue!" Remember, you want to have kids rely on a repertoire of strategies they have learned to bring their characters to life. So it will be important to encourage kids to do more than just add dialogue. As you send them off in your link, invite them to try all the strategies they know to add to their stories.

CONFERRING AND SMALL-GROUP WORK

In a small group today, you might work with some of your strongest writers on extending their dialogue so that it moves the story along. You might show them, for example, how "Hi, what's up?" sounds realistic, but "Hey, stop fooling around!" builds story tension. The truth is most writers exaggerate their dialogue to add drama to a story. Invite children to role-play some dialogue that would make Charles feel ashamed or upset. "You need to be more careful," or "You cannot ride your skateboard anymore," Charles's father might say to him, or "I can't believe you were so foolish!"

   Another possibility is to pull a small group whom you are concerned need to look at what is actually happening in their story, and how each part makes sense in terms of the whole story. In other words, does the dialogue add to the story or confuse the reader? For these writers, you might remind partners of questions they have learned to ask each other. For example, Who? Where? When? What? How? Answering those questions leads writers to add more specific details to their pieces. It also helps them keep their reader in mind, or at least help them write stories that make sense. Another helpful technique is to have partners switch stories, and read each other's stories out loud. Hearing someone else read their story sometimes helps writers realize when parts or words are missing.

MID-WORKSHOP TEACHING

During your mid-workshop teaching, you might want to emphasize that writers don't only bring their stories to life by using dialogue and actions; they also include what is happening on the inside of the characters— their feelings. You may recall the reference mentioned in the Small Moments unit: writers think about what is in their character's heart and mind. This will help them to add thinking and feeling as well as talking and doing! Look for a student who is edging toward this work, or doing it well. If it's the former, help him or her develop the feelings in their piece and then share this good work with the whole class. If it's the latter, you're all ready to shine a spotlight on this student's work as a model.

SHARE

For the share today, you might invite children to bring out their favorite story so far, and pair up with a partner or a small group. Then, they might rehearse and act out their stories together, using each other as actors. Encourage them to take on voices for the dialogue, to use their bodies to act out the part of the slug or the dog—to really enjoy bringing their stories to life for an audience.

   We wish you joy,
   Christine and Mary

① Name Autumn   Date 4-30

One sprin day syony and her frend
rdeco wroe playing a game and
then we saw something...

② Name Autumn   Date 4-30

IT WAS A Slung!!!!! we all
gasps.

③ Name Autumn   Date 4-30

I DoD
like slugs!!!

then te wec sta did lo ran a way
and yelled I DODt LIKE
SLUGS!!!!!

④ Name Autumn   Date 4-30

Then Seyon said "come no its
gust a slug." redecay crept a
little clasr

⑤ Name Autumn   Date 5-3

seyh said "come on lets look at
the snal." rdecay said "oka I will
chriy not to dy scord."

FIG. 8–1   Children might choose a story to read aloud to their writing buddies, or read each other's stories in small "read-aloud" groups, doing their best dramatic read, with attention to dialogue and punctuation. Asking writers to read their writing aloud helps emphasize the significance of ending punctuation, especially. Here you see Autumn punctuating her dialogue and sentences to guide her reader.

Session 9

Saddle Up to the Revision Party— and Bring Your Favorite Writer

I N THIS FINAL SESSION before the mid-unit celebration, you'll invite students to tackle revision in both the stories they've written so far and in new stories they decide to write. The work in this session and the following one will include using tools such as mentor texts, the narrative writing checklists, and editing checklists. You may want to think through the logistics of this work before embarking on teaching the content. Will you copy these tools for students, or simply show them on chart paper or an overhead? What systems should students practice for incorporating revision?

Until now, your writers have probably been adding words to their pages, and pages to their booklets. It might be that simply adding words to pages and pages to booklets will suffice. Or it might be that you want to begin to introduce colored pencils for small changes, or folded flaps, or the revision strips that many second grade teachers call spider legs, so that children can revise individual pages. You may want to find out what expectations teachers in the next grade have, or what they would love for you to have introduced, in terms of children managing revisions. It doesn't seem worth it for first graders to copy over their books, but they could "give them a shine" as they approach the publication of their first series.

At some point in the next two days, you'll also want to begin the "boxed set" process, inviting students to bring cereal boxes in from home, painting these, adding pictures of the author or illustrations, getting ready for publishing. Simultaneously working on the craft of the finished project often keeps children's energy high for the revision work they need to do. After all, for such a beautiful boxed set, you want all the parts of your story to shine, you'll suggest.

If you haven't thought through your celebration yet, now is a good time to do a little thinking about it in case you want to send out invitations, partner with another class, or reserve the library. One option is to wait for the very end of the unit, when students will have two boxed sets of series, as a time to invite parents in, celebrate the authors, add their series to the library, and generally have the kind of gala that writers love when they have been working hard for many weeks. Another option, though, is to do that,

IN THIS SESSION, you'll launch a "revision party," and you'll suggest that writers invite their favorite author as an honored guest.

GETTING READY

✔ Writing center stocked with revision supplies: pens, strips, flaps, tape, extra paper, and so on

✔ Sign that welcomes students to a revision party (see Connection)

✔ Your own writing folder with the fiction books you've written, to be brought to the meeting area

✔ Students' writing folders, to be brought to the meeting area

✔ A mentor text you have selected, such as *Henry and Mudge and the Happy Cat.* You will need one mentor text for your demonstration and enough copies of additional mentor texts (we use other Henry and Mudge books) for kids to share during the active engagement.

✔ "Our Favorite Series Authors . . ." chart, to add things you and your class notice from the mentor texts (see Teaching, Active Engagement, and Conferring)

✔ Children's favorite fiction books from reading workshop (see Conferring and Share)

COMMON CORE STATE STANDARDS: W.1.3, W.1.5, W.1.7, W.1.8, W.2.3, RL.1.1, RL.1.2, RL.1.3, RL.1.4, RL.1.7, RL.1.10, SL.1.1, L.1.1, L.1.2

but also plan something small for publishing children's first series. We recommend partnering with a kindergarten class and inviting children to read their stories aloud in their best read-aloud voice, perhaps followed by children having time to move around their own classroom, reading each other's stories. It's always good for writers to know that someone else will be reading their writing. That provides the impetus for neater handwriting, better spelling, and more attention to punctuation. Thinking ahead, then, means that you can set up expectations for your first publishing party. The combination of those expectations, and children's excitement over getting a "boxed set" ready, should fuel your children's energy for revision.

One of the implicit purposes of the revision and elaboration work in this session is to suggest that revision work is fun, that writers who revise are daring, and that this is one of the good parts of writing. The attitudes you instill in your writers may stay with them for many years, so *how* you act about going back into your own writing is as important as *what* you do to revise.

In this session, you'll have students study some of the details and sentences of mentor texts in order to emulate that work, really teaching students how to read as writers. They'll be going back into stories they've written so far, but we also hope that they will carry this thinking into new stories, as revision strategies eventually become drafting strategies. Today, though, you are showing your writers that they can learn from professional writers.

"The attitudes you instill in your writers may stay with them for many years, so how you act about going back into your own writing is as important as what you do to revise."

Saddle Up to the Revision Party— and Bring Your Favorite Writer

CONNECTION

◆ COACHING

Stir up your writers into thinking of their drafts as invitations to a revision party.

"Writers, last night I was watching an old western movie with cowboys. At one point in the movie, the cowboys were going to a party. The cowboys kept saying, 'Saddle up, partner! It's time to get to that party!' I love that expression. Saddle up! In fact, this morning when it was time to take my dog for a walk, I said to her, 'Saddle Up! It's time for walkies!'" The kids began to giggle and whisper "Saddle up" to each other.

I looked intently at the children and said, "It's time for us to saddle up and get to a party, writers. It's time to saddle up for a *revision* party."

I held up a little sign that said:

> Welcome to the Revision Party! Saddle Up and Come on In!
> Cynthia Rylant will be an honored guest!

As the children stared, I explained, "A revision party is when writers get together and start having a good time adding new stuff to their stories." I took out my stories from my folder. "Our stories are our invitations to the revision party.

"Writers, I'm holding in my hands my invitation to the revision party. Can you show your partner your invitation? When you see your partner is holding his or her stories, you can say, 'You've got your invitation to the party, partner! Saddle up!'"

Giggling, the kids pulled out their stories, telling each other, "Saddle up! We've got a party to go to!"

"All right, partners, I can see you all have your invitations to the revision party. Now let's see what happens at the party. Saddle up!"

Inventing memorable language is how you create lasting metaphors in your classroom. Here, we create the "Revision Party" as a replicable event, and "Saddle Up" as the invitation.

We've mentioned before that attitude matters when it comes to revision. Remember that attitude is catching. If you act like revision will be fun, that this is a good part of writing, then your children will follow along in the same manner. If you slip into "I know it's hard, but you need to . . ." or "You really have to fix . . ." then your children will conceptualize revision as something unpleasant. The metaphor you're launching today is one that Roy Peter Clark modeled in a writing workshop at Teachers College. We thought it was delightful, and have used it with writers of all ages, since.

Name the teaching point.

"Writers, the idea of a revision party is to have fun together, finding ways to make your fiction books sparkle. One way writers figure out ways to add sparkle to *their* fiction books is to see what kinds of things their favorite authors put in their books."

TEACHING

Demonstrate how writers revisit a favorite mentor text, pointing to favorite pages and naming something they like that they could add to their own stories.

I picked up a favorite Henry and Mudge story. "Writers, I'm going to look at just a few pages of a couple of Henry and Mudge stories. Maybe Cynthia Rylant will give me some new ideas for how to add onto my story. I think you already know how to do this work as well, so start collecting your own ideas as we read."

"Hmm." I flipped slowly through the pages of *Henry and Mudge and the Happy Cat*, reading aloud as I went, putting my finger on parts that stood out, and jotting some ideas on a chart. I read, "One night, Henry and Henry's father and Henry's big dog Mudge were watching TV." I put my finger on the page with the picture. "And there's a picture of Henry and his dog and father all curled up on a pink couch. It looks really comfortable. Cynthia Rylant really gives you some clues about the setting—where the story happens—both in her words and in her illustrations. Her pictures of the living room add sparkle to the story. I can almost hear the TV and feel Mudge sitting on me!" I jotted that on a chart.

Then I picked up the book again. "What else does Cynthia Rylant do? Is there anything else I think is a good idea for me as a writer? Let's see." I read on a little bit and then pointed to a new page.

"I guess I really like the way she says, 'Suddenly, Mudge ran.' There's something kind of scary. It really gets your attention. I was afraid it might be a burglar! I guess I can say she makes the action exciting." I added that to the chart so that it now read:

> Our Favorite Series Authors . . .
>
> - Describe the setting (the place, the weather, the season, the time of day)
> - Make the action exciting!

please join us...

It's time for us to saddle up and get to a party, writers. It's time to saddle up for a revision party.

Where: School
When: Now!
Who: Writers
Why: revision is fun!

When we see that an author has used the same technique in various places, we can begin to envision the technique as transferable to our own texts. In any author study, even if the author doesn't use the technique multiple times in one text, I ask students to find other instances of the same technique by asking, "Where else have you seen an author use this technique?"

ACTIVE ENGAGEMENT

Give students an opportunity to revisit some pages of a favorite series book. Encourage them to point to one favorite page at a time and name one thing the author puts in the story. Capture the results of their research.

"Writers, let's give you a chance to try this. I've put some Henry and Mudge books in front of you. Why don't you look at one with a few writers near you. When you see a part that you like, put your finger on it, and name one thing Cynthia Rylant does in her book that you can do in your own fiction book. I'll try to capture what you say to add to our list."

I distributed some books. As the children pointed to parts they liked, I helped them name those parts as things they could do in their own stories. I generalized their observations.

Rosa said, "I like the way there's a picture just of the cat on this page, and it shows how scruffy he is."

I said, "Yes, that is good. So Cynthia Rylant puts a picture or a lot of details about new characters."

Alejandra put her finger on two pages, and said, 'Cynthia Rylant makes Henry worry a lot! He worried here . . . and here . . . and here . . . "

"Oh," I said, "so you see a pattern. That's so interesting." I added those to our chart, along with other craft moves I heard after listening in to other writers. Then I convened the children.

"Writers, can I have your eyes up here please? I bet when you see all the ideas we got from Cynthia Rylant, you're going to be dying to add some of these things to your fiction books. Give a thumbs up whenever we get to something you'd love to try." I pointed to the chart and read.

> - Give a lot of details for new characters
> - Add special details to their pictures
> - Make a pattern ("he worried about . . . he worried that . . . mostly he worried . . . ")

"Writers, I can see from how often you've been putting your thumbs up that you have a lot of ideas. Some of you want to add all these things! Isn't it great we invited Cynthia Rylant to our revision party?"

You might distribute some copies of books from the Henry and Mudge series, as these are familiar. Pretty much, though, your children will be able to do this work in any highly accessible text. Be sure the pictures invite analysis to support all your students, not just your strong readers.

If a child names what the author has done, give the child the ultimate compliment of learning from the child's observation, as I do when I say, "You know what? You're right! Wow!" instead of complimenting the child for the right answer (for example, "Good for you"). You could also follow up by asking, "Where do you see that?" Ask as if the child is informing you and others (rather than asking the child in a "Can you guess the right answer?" sort of way).

LINK

Send students off, tucking in some cues so they'll apply strategies you taught earlier, such as giving themselves orders, getting their own supplies, choosing more than one part and more than one book to add onto.

"Saddle up, writers! It's time to start our revision party! Today I'm hoping that before you start a new book, you'll take some time to go back into the stories you've written so far, and give them added sparkle, by doing some of the work that you loved in Cynthia Rylant's story. Think of those boxed sets you'll be publishing, and how you want every book in them to be fabulous.

"Let me give you some tips to help you get started. One, you might want to think about how to fit all these additions in. Do you want to tape in a whole new page? Do you want to make flaps or little strips? Those supplies are ready for you. Two, you might want your mentor text at your table. Lots of writers like to have a favorite book next to them as they revise, to inspire them. Three, I bet you were going to give directions to yourself, to plan your work. You should also tell your partner your plans, so later you can check in with each other and see how it's going. Off you go!"

Sometimes, it's helpful in the link to describe the logistics of the work—in this case, the decisions to be made about flaps or strips or added pages. Otherwise children might have ideas for writing but get stuck on these details.

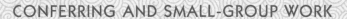

Pulling Readers to Do Mentor Text Work on Their Leveled Texts

ON THIS DAY, you may decide to pull some of your lower-level readers together during your conferring and small-group time if the Henry and Mudge books are a high reach for them as writers. What better mentors than the books they read! They probably know them by heart.

To organize this small group, you can invite a group of kids to the meeting area with their writing folders (their invitation to the party) and their bag of independent reading books. Have pens, strips, tape, and extra paper nearby.

I began my small group on this day by saying, "Today you all looked at Henry and Mudge books together, and you got so many revision ideas that you could use in your fiction books. That got me thinking that you all have baggies *full* of books you read during reading workshop, and these books may be helpful for you during writing workshop too!

"Okay, you know how to learn from mentor authors. Go ahead. Choose a book from your baggie that you want to look at more closely. As you read it over, remember to stop if you find a place you love, a place you want to be like the author, a place you see something you can try too." You'll notice I repeated the task, using many different phrases, and I pointed to favorite pages in the books as I did so, acting as if they knew how to do this but giving extra cues as well.

Within seconds kids were calling out, eager to share what they saw. They already had favorite parts in these familiar books.

Ethan said, "Look in my book, *Tiny and the Big Wave*. The family shouts, 'COME BACK TINY!' The words are so big, like the POP-OUT words we learned in Unit 1, *Small Moments*."

Other kids started saying, "Mine has big, bold POP-OUT words too!"

MID-WORKSHOP TEACHING   Writers Stretch Themselves by Adding a Lot of Sentences When They Add to Their Fiction Books

"Writers, eyes up here." I waited until I had everyone's attention. "I want to show you something Justin has done. Justin was looking at the Henry and Mudge book, *Henry and Mudge and the Happy Cat*, because it's his favorite." I held it up. "I was walking by when I saw that Justin had jotted a Post-it: 'ADD 4 DETAILS.' And he had it stuck to a page of his fiction book. When I asked him, 'What's this?' Justin explained that he wanted to add details about a new character in his story, so he gave himself orders to add as many details as Cynthia Rylant added about her new character. Four new details! It's great the way Justin gave himself orders, and he really tried to stretch himself as a writer by adding a lot of new details in one part of his fiction book.

"You might show your partner where are you working hard too, and adding at least three or four new sentences."

In a rush of excitement, Zoe pulled out her own story, and pointed to where she had tried this technique. Her character, Gigi, screamed, "**Cat come back**" in big, bold pop-out words! (See Figure 9–1.)

You can often take what kids say and name it so that it becomes a strategy they can do in their own writing too. For instance, "Writers make their letters big to make the dialogue *loud*!"

(continues)

FIG. 9–1 Zoe uses "pop-out" words to create exciting dialogue.

Miles noticed in his book, *The Hungry Kitten*, there was a picture of a kitten all alone with his head down. Again, exploring why the author did that, the kids clearly stated that they can draw pictures that exaggerate how a character feels and what they are doing.

Ethan noticed in his book, *Worm Builds*, that worm keeps building a tower on every page. "It's a pattern. Worm builds a tower on every page, and it keeps falling," he said.

Together we thought about it and decided some books may have things in both pictures and words that repeat.

You may decide to add what the kids noticed from their own books to the "Our Favorite Series Authors . . . " chart.

Our Favorite Series Authors . . .

- Describe the setting (the place, the weather, the season, the time of day)
- Make the action exciting!
- Give a lot of details for new characters
- Add special details to their pictures
- Make a pattern ("he worried about . . . he worried that . . . mostly he worried . . . ")
- Add POP-OUT words
- Show characters' strong feelings in pictures
- Repeat action in pictures and words

Later, you might use this chart as part of your share.

Using Mentor Texts for Revision Ideas

Suggest to your writers that they don't have to wait for a teacher to find mentor texts. Tell them they walk through the world differently because they are readers who write and writers who read.

"Writers, can you come to the meeting area, and can you bring your book baggies?" I waited for them to settle in. "Eyes on me. Ethan and his writing friends over here have done some work that I think could be helpful for all of us. You know how we all looked at Henry and Mudge together and thought about what Cynthia Rylant could teach us as writers? Well, Ethan and his buddies realized they could invite other writers to the revision party! They brought along some of their special favorites from their book baggies. And look at how we added to the 'Our Favorite Series Authors . . .' chart with the new ideas they got from them.

"I'll bet you might want to invite some of the authors you have in your baggies to the party. Right now, can you pull out a book that you've read, think for a moment about a part you liked, and then find that part?" I waited in silence for children to find their parts. "Now, tell your partner, what's something this author does that you really like? And where would you want to do that work in your story? Go ahead, talk with your partner. Make some serious plans."

The children put their fingers on places in the books they were reading and the books they were writing. Their noticings were big and small, from "make a fancy title," or "number the pages," to "show strong feelings with big words."

"Writers, eyes on me again. Listen, there's one thing I have to tell you right now. It's that you are each making writing plans, and some of the writing work you are planning I didn't teach you! Cynthia Rylant taught you, or James Howe, or another author. The only one now who knows these writing plans is your partner. That means it's going to be extra important to show each other what you're doing. Only your partner will really know what you were planning, and how it's going. So before we stop, make sure you know what your partner is planning."

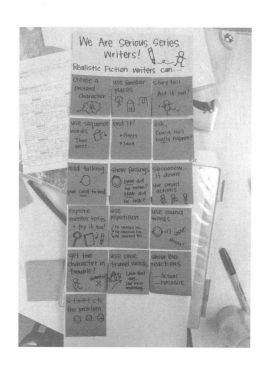

Celebrating Our First Series

𝔇ear Teachers,

Congratulations. Your children are series writers! By now our hope is that you and your students are not only serious about series writing but also are having a lot of fun doing it. Today we are suggesting that you have a mid-unit celebration as kids finish up their first series. Even though they will be continuing to work on realistic fiction series over the next two bends, it is important to recognize the work and growth your students have achieved at this point in the unit. After all their hard work, there is a lot to celebrate. Here are some ideas. You may decide to have them "saddle up" for an editing party. You may also give some time to decorate the boxes for those "boxed sets," with pictures and blurbs about the author. The combination of editing with something highly creative should get your kids revved up to publish their first series. As each story gets edited, they can add it to their box.

You may recall a favorite boxed set you had as a young reader. We can vividly picture our E. B. White boxed sets sitting on our shelves in our childhood bedrooms. There was something so enticing about how the three books—*Charlotte's Web*, *Stuart Little*, and *The Trumpet of the Swan*—looked tucked together in a beautifully illustrated box. Later, we had a boxed set of the Misty of Chincoteague series, and Nancy Drew, and Lord of the Rings.

So as part of this celebration you might put out some boxed sets as mentors, so your kids can see what they want to add to their own. Their boxed sets can then sit on your library shelves honoring the work all your students did and be available for others to enjoy. It will mark the first famous series by these authors! If you haven't yet, you might want to gather and bring in cereal boxes, construction paper, glue, scissors, tape, markers, ribbons, or anything else you can think of to help your writers celebrate in style.

To tackle final editing, you can have kids use what they know about editing, refer to the Narrative Writing Checklist, or use an editing checklist that they have used throughout the year for the editing portion of the workshop. Certainly by now they can edit for beginning and ending punctuation, capital letters of names, spelling of high-frequency words, and legibility.

COMMON CORE STATE STANDARDS: W.1.3, W.1.5. W.2.3, RL.1.1, RL.1.3, RFS.1.4, SL.1.1, SL.1.6, L.1.1, L.1.2

MINILESSON

In your connection you may actually show the kids some boxed sets from published authors to create a vision and build enthusiasm. You can teach that writers make sure their work is as finished as possible before they send it out into the world. That means making sure that the writing is easy to read and the presentation is beautiful. Then invite the children to choose a few stories they have written in the past two weeks to edit and fancy up and put into a decorated box of their very own.

It may seem like a lofty job but remember, they have edited before, have shared their writing with their partners all throughout the writing process already, and are motivated to do arts and crafts projects. So keep the pace moving.

During your demonstration, you might refer to your editing checklist to help kids decide how they can fix up their writing so it is ready to celebrate and share with others. See the sample checklist below as an example. This checklist can also be found on the CD-ROM.

My Editing Checklist

✓ I put spaces between my words.
✓ I checked the word wall.
✓ I spelled tricky words the best I can. I wrote letters for most of the sounds.
✓ I used ending punctuation and capital letters to start sentences.
✓ I can read my writing, and my friend can read most of my writing without my help.
✓ I started my character's name with a capital letter.

When you demonstrate, be sure you exaggerate how you *reread* your writing to find places to edit to make your writing more readable.

You can also model writing titles for a few of your demonstration books. For example, "Gretchen Builds the Tree Fort," "Gretchen Finds a Baby Animal," and "Gretchen and the Big Storm." Then your boxed set might be called, "The Gretchen Series." Or even "The Famous Gretchen Series."

Finally, you may want to have a cereal box of your own painted and decorated and ready to show to students to serve as an example. Keep in mind that kids will have creative ways of their own to add details to their box, so there's no need to walk through this step by step. Often simply supplying materials is enough. Soon you'll see them putting prices, adding publisher's awards, and so on.

For today's active engagement you may have the kids bring their folders to the meeting area so that right then and there they can select a few stories they will celebrate and put in their boxed set. Perhaps when they turn and talk to a partner they can make a plan for the day's work ahead.

You can send kids off today armed with a plan and the materials needed to make a boxed set ready for your classroom library.

CONFERRING AND SMALL-GROUP WORK

During independent writing time you will most likely be doing lots of coaching and complimenting. You may also decide to pull partnerships to form a small group with a focus on rereading to see if the story sounds right, looks right, and makes sense, just as they do when they read just-right books. Often, it's helpful for the partner to read the other partner's story aloud, as it can be hard for a writer to catch gaps and missing parts as she reads her own writing. When she hears her story read aloud by her partner, though, she often hears the missing parts.

MID-WORKSHOP TEACHING

You may want to remind children that as they are getting ready to celebrate, if they want to make revisions in addition to edits they can feel free to do that too. You might say, "Remember, editing is fixing spelling, grammar, and conventions. Revision is adding more and making changes to the writing. Sometimes writers suddenly see that they want to add a flap or a page to add to their story. Go for it!"

SHARE

If you've arranged it, your students can then take their boxed sets to the library for a celebration, or bring a story to a kindergarten classroom to read aloud. Today is a good time to invite kids to do a professional-type read-aloud with one of their stories, whether that is with a younger child, with a partner, or in small groups. Or perhaps you'll choose one and do an accountable talk read-aloud, complete with think-alouds and opportunities for partner talk and whole-class conversation. You can decide on a few reading skills you want to highlight, such as prediction, inferring, and maybe even interpretation of the big idea or lesson learned! The kids really get a kick out of doing the same thinking and talking they do on a book like *Henry and Mudge and the Happy Cat* as they do on their own writing. And what a great teaching opportunity for explicit reading and writing connections.

   As kids finish, place the boxed sets in your library. Keep in mind that some kids may decide to finish their box at home or another time of day.

   Congratulations, writers!

   Christine and Mary

FIG. 10–1   A student's boxed set. The making of a boxed set really honors the children's writing.

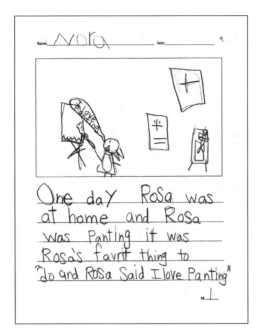

Name: Nora   Date: 9

One day Rosa was
at home and Rosa
was Panting it was
Rosa's favrit thing to
"do and Rosa Said I love Panting"

pg 1

Name: Nora   Date:

Rosa Pantid a Picchr of
a tree and gras it was
a butafl Panting.

pg 2

Name: Nora   Date:

But then the babby
sister came in Rosa's
room and mest up the
"Panting and Rosa said"
"nOOOOW!!!!!"

pg 3

Name: Nora   Date:

Then Rosa's Mom came
"and Said wat is going on"
"and Rosa Said my babby"
Sister mest up my Picchr"

pg 4

Name: Nora   Date:

Then Rosa that hardr intll Rosa
new wat Rosa that that her
litll sister wantid to Pant to and
she did the end.

pg 5

FIG. 10–2   One of Nora's revised stories for her boxed set

①

Name: Zoe   Date:

Gigi at School

Gigi was goin to School
with her cat. She was
Happ Because it was
Sowinteli.

②

Name: Date:

Then Gigi's loses her cat.
She Skrem̃d, ~~MY CAT~~
Come back

her cat ~~N~~ Did ^not^ come back.

③

Name: Date:

Gigi Look and Look for
the cat. She Did not fid
the cat. She Look Next to the
Bookis, and She Look Next to
the Art rome.

④

Name: Date:

Then ~~~~ She Fid the cat
in the Lunch rome.
The cat ran a way Because,
The cat had Baby's.

⑤

Name: Date:

Last Gigi's cat had Baby.
~~~~ She had tow Baby.

FIG. 10–3   One of Zoe's revised stories for her boxed set

Becoming More Powerful at Realistic Fiction: Studying the Genre and Studying Ourselves as Writers

Series Writers Investigate What Makes Realistic Fiction Realistic

IN THIS SESSION, you'll teach students that writers call on their own experiences to imagine the tiny, authentic details that make realistic fiction seem so real.

GETTING READY

✔ A few fiction books from two different series written by the same author (for example, Henry and Mudge and Mr. Putter and Tabby) to show students that when authors finish one series, they set out to write another one

✔ Mentor text, in our case *Henry and Mudge and the Happy Cat.* You will need pages identified that demonstrate realistic qualities to use in the teaching part of the minilesson.

✔ Charts you have been using throughout the unit to highlight in the link ("How to Write a Realistic Fiction Book" from Session 1; "How to Write Series Books" from Session 6; "Ways to Bring Stories to Life" from Unit 1, *Small Moments*; "Our Favorite Series Authors . . . " from Session 9)

✔ Writing center stocked with various paper choices to match your writers. You may have some with more lines and some with all lines and no picture box.

✔ Post-its for students to write down their work goals

COMMON CORE STATE STANDARDS: W.1.3, W.1.5, W.1.8, W.2.3, RL.1.1, RL.1.2, RL.1.3, SL.1.1, SL.1.4, SL.1.5, L.1.1, L.1.2

Whenever we are teaching writing, we are alert for moments when we can clearly demarcate opportunities for transference; that is, we look for opportunities to raise the level of work to what Norman Webb describes in his research as Depth of Knowledge (DOK), Level 4—when kids carry what they've learned into fresh situations, applying what they've learned with more agency. This is one of those moments. Your children have completed one whole cycle of the writing process, developing several stories from start to finish, with you teaching them some new moves as writers and reinforcing some essentials. Now they'll have the opportunity to launch the whole cycle again, so that they have a chance to internalize those strategies and to put them into play with more efficiency as well as more independence. This means that some strategies that you taught over more than one session you'll now expect your writers to do automatically, converging several strategies at once to get started powerfully.

In this first session of the bend, your children will have a chance to show off their prowess as series writers by using what they know to come up with a pretend character and some trouble for that character, rehearse their story using a method of their choice, and start writing on paper that will stretch them as writers. All those skills, you'll suggest, are now a given. Across all the sessions of this bend, as you teach the students *new* strategies as series writers, it's helpful to demarcate what is *not* new. One way to do that is to develop an attitude of "use all that you know," and "I'm going to admire you as . . . " High expectations matter.

Today, then, you'll want to set the bar high. Just as a soccer coach expects her players to know what to do on the second day of practice and to understand more about team rituals after a couple of games, you need to visibly show your faith in your students and your high expectations for them. This time, therefore, you will not teach them how to get started as writers. What you will do is narrow their focus to realistic fiction—to that particular kind of fiction that feels true to life. This is large-scale work that focuses on putting aside the aliens and monsters. In the next session, you'll focus more attentively to the piling up of tiny, realistic details.

One could question, of course, whether it really matters what kind of fiction children write, as long as they are doing a lot of writing and working on structure, craft, convention, and process. For students who seem disengaged except when they can write about aliens, of course you can bypass this focus on realistic versus other kinds of fiction. For most of your writers, though, this gives you a chance to introduce two important skills related to writing within a genre. The first is that writers think not just about the type of writing they are pursuing, but the specific genre, and they study what makes that genre powerful. The second skill is that writers decide what to include and not include in their writing based on their knowledge of the genre, and when you decide to leave some stuff (like aliens) out, it leaves you more energy to develop what you leave in (realistic characters).

"Schoolyard stories, playground stories, family adventures—children can write about these with great authenticity and detail, as well as true meaning."

Some of this focus on realistic fiction arises from long experience that young writers may write more when writing about aliens, but they rarely write better. Schoolyard stories, playground stories, family adventures—children can write about these with great authenticity and detail, as well as true meaning. The real emotions that underlie so many of their daily interactions seep through their childish drawings and rough spelling, with many moments of true unhappiness, fear, joy, and love—the truly great stuff of stories.

Series Writers Investigate What Makes Realistic Fiction Realistic

CONNECTION

Celebrate the series work students have done so far as a means of extolling their new powers that they'll put into play soon.

"Writers, this is such an exciting morning. I look around at your first published series in boxed sets, and I realize that I am in the company of true authors. In fact, just for a moment, go ahead and shake hands with someone near you, and give an author introduction. Make it sound like Cynthia Rylant might if she were introducing herself." I put out my hand, saying, "Hi, I'm Cynthia. I'm the author of the Henry and Mudge series."

The kids did this. There was a chorus of "I'm Mohammad. I'm the author of the Pablo series," and "I wrote a series about a boy named Joshua."

I held up some of Cynthia Rylant's Henry and Mudge books and a few Mr. Putter and Tabby books. "Writers, you know what Cynthia Rylant did right after finishing her first series?" I waited a moment for the children to whisper, "She wrote another one!"

"That's right, children, Cynthia wrote another series! Because she knew her readers wanted more! And because she was getting so good at it! It's kind of like riding a bike, or playing an instrument, or learning baseball. Once you learn how, you want to keep doing it! When you learn to throw a baseball, you want to throw, and throw, and throw. When you become a fiction writer, you want to write, and write and write.

"So we're going to get a chance to do that. Today you'll have a chance to show off everything you know about getting started with a fiction series, because you've written a lot of series books now. Before we start, though, I'm going to invite you to really think about what makes realistic fiction . . . realistic. We already know that fiction means the writer gets to pretend, but what about the realistic part?"

❖ **Name the teaching point.**

"Today I want to teach you that realistic fiction writers often study what makes realistic fiction seem so realistic. Then they call on their own experiences to write stories that seem this real."

Be sure to take opportunities along the way to commemorate hard work. Also, by naming the children as series authors, you role-play them into the role of writers. Alfred Tatum and Pedro Noguera, who both research the struggle between peer culture and academic culture, note how important it is that all children take up roles that are academic.

Every time you make comparisons to activities that children work hard at, such as baseball, or music, or bike-riding, you explicitly suggest that children want to get better at things, including writing. In Outliers (2011), Malcolm Gladwell speaks of the famous 10,000 hours that differentiate high achievers. Seize every opportunity to reinforce the joy of working at becoming better at something.

TEACHING

Return to your mentor text, in our case, *Henry and Mudge and the Happy Cat*. Initiate a mini-inquiry into what makes some fiction feel so real. Later, you'll debrief in ways that young writers can copy.

"Writers, to figure out what authors do to make stories seem real—to make them 'realistic fiction,' let's take a look back at one of our favorites, *Henry and Mudge and the Happy Cat*. Watch me as I turn the pages and read a little. As I read, ask yourself this question: 'What feels real about this story?' I'll think about that question as well."

I picked up the book and read the first few pages, showing the students the pictures as I did so. "What feels real about this story? Well, right away, one thing that feels real is the place—the way this story starts in Henry's house. It's not on a spaceship or inside a volcano." The children giggled. "And I guess another thing that feels very realistic is that the characters are ordinary people who do ordinary things. Look at this picture. It's a boy, his dad, and his dog. Henry and his father are wearing ordinary clothes, and they are watching TV on the couch. This feels very real to me as a reader. And then, of course, the TV doesn't turn into an alien and try to kill them! Instead, Mudge hears a noise at the door and starts barking. Henry's like a real dog!"

I turned to the children. "Do you see how I'm asking myself that question, 'What feels real about this story?' I'm noticing the choices that Cynthia Rylant made. The family, the way they are on the couch, and the TV, and the dog barking at the door. Were you noticing those details too? Already, in my mind, Cynthia Rylant's choices are giving me ideas for making my fiction books more realistic."

ACTIVE ENGAGEMENT

Give students a chance to revisit a few more pages, listening in as they notice realistic details, and voicing over to help name them.

"Let's give you a chance to try this. I'm going to read a few more pages and show you some of the pictures. As I read, try to notice the details that are realistic. Start with your hand in a fist. Whenever you notice one, put up a thumb, and when I pause, you and your partner can compare what you noticed. I'm going to read from the next chapter, after Henry and his dad have taken the cat in."

I read a few pages, starting with Chapter 2, "A Good Mother." As I did so, children began to put thumbs up in the air. "Go ahead, partners, turn and talk." I listened in and nodded, making comparisons to what was *not* in the story for emphasis. "Yes, the next thing that happens is the cat loves living with them, and the things the cat loves are so real—the towel closet, the bath tub, and Mudge! It's not like the cat turns into a ninja or leaves in a spaceship and everyone cries. There's a realistic, happy part, when the cat just loves the house!" I turned to another partnership and listened in. "Oh yes, you're right, the cat does real cat things. Cats do lick other animals! So the cat doesn't turn into a monster—she does cat things."

Once again, the technique of compare and contrast will help children to clarify their task. In this case, you'll contrast the realistic quality of fiction by giving an example of what feels real (watching TV on the couch) with what wouldn't feel real (aliens and volcanoes). Imagining what your mentor author could have written, or didn't write, can be an effective technique for focusing children's attention on the author's decisions.

The ninjas and spaceships will have your kids giggling—and will also help them ponder if they have these elements in their realistic fiction.

Debrief, summarizing what students have noticed, transforming their details into broader generalizations.

"Writers, I love how you really thought about this question, 'What feels real about this story?' and that let you zoom in on the author's choices. Like you noticed the way there are *real animals*, and the animals do animal things, like the cat licks everyone, and lies in the towels. Now we can really see why Cynthia Rylant's stories are *realistic* fiction. Everything is realistic, from the cat who licks, to the family snuggled up to the TV, to the way Henry has to lie down when he's sad. Every part of the story feels so real."

LINK

Recall some of the steps fiction writers follow, and remind students of tools that are in the room to help them, telling them that they can and need to apply what they know to get started independently.

"Writers, you know how to get started with a new series. There are some charts here that you can study with your partner to help you get started if you want. And you know stuff we don't even have charts for anymore, like finding your own paper and a place to write, and getting a lot of work done. I'm going to admire you as you do the thinking and writing work of beginning a new series about a new character. As you do this work, add in what you learned today from Cynthia Rylant, about making every part of the story feel real."

Once again, this unit of study leads your students to be analytic readers as well as prolific writers. Here, your students sharpen their awareness of genre characteristics.

Rehearsing Leads as a Way to Practice Authorial Choices

AS YOUR STUDENTS settle in to rehearse a new series and a new story, you might consider conferring with some students around leads. Your first graders already know something about different ways to start a story—what you'll really want to work on then is that they make an authorial choice, to move beyond "whatever I thought of." Just as authors make choices about making a story realistic, they also make choices about how to start a story, and some of your writers will be ready for that work. Izzy, for instance, was planning out her story as I settled in beside her. "I'm glad to see you've chosen paper with so many lines on it, Izzy," I said, noting the small picture box and lots of lines. Izzy was a prolific writer. She often wrote fast and furious, and I was eager to help her begin to think harder about making choices as a writer. "Izzy," I continued. "I see you're about to start writing. You have your sketches filled in, and you're just about to put your pencil to paper. Have you thought yet about how

your story will begin?" Izzy immediately began to tell me about what would happen in her story. "Izzy," I stopped her. "I'm not asking what will happen in your story, I'm asking about *how* your story will start. What choice are you making as a writer? Is this Book One, and are you going to introduce your character with lots of details? Is this a later book, and you'll start with action? What choice will you make as a writer?" Izzy pondered for a moment, and I suggested she do a little more thinking.

A few moments later I heard Izzy tell her partner that she had decided to make this story Book One, and that she would start by introducing "Katie, who was ten years old, who lived in Mexico, who had no dad, and who never lied." "That sounds like a

---

Name: Izzy   Date: _____

```
Hello! My Name is Katie. I live in
Mexico. I never lie and always tell the
truth. I have no dad but I have a
Mom Named rebecca. yesterday I took
a airplane to hawii. we are staying
in a hut on the beach.today im
going swimming. I'M leaving on Saturday
and today is wensday. my mom
said that in the afternoon I'm going
swimming in the deep ocean. Im ten
years old.
```

FIG. 11–1 Izzy recalls the strategy of introducing a character in Book One of a series, and deploys it here, independently.

MID-WORKSHOP TEACHING
Writers Get Started Writing in Different Ways

"Writers, can I stop you and tell you what I have been noticing about you all as writers? I think you will find this really interesting! Eyes on me." I waited until I had everyone's attention. "You have become such independent writers, and I noticed that many of you do different things to get started writing."

I pointed to various writers as I described their processes. "Listen to this. I noticed ways you tell your story to get ready. Nora tells it across her fingers, Avery tells it across pages, and Annabel likes to tell it to her partner. Then I noticed a few things some of you do to help you remember your story. Miles likes to sketch a little picture first, Serenity writes an important word on each page, and Robert prefers to write an entire sentence on each page saying what will happen in each part. I even saw Mohammad and Sophia ready to just start writing without a picture box! So, next time you get started writing, think about which way works for you. It's great that you are figuring out how to get your best work done!"

fascinating character, Izzy!" I said as I listened in. "I like the way you told all those details about her across your fingers. I can't wait to meet Katie in Book One, and follow her adventures in all your stories."

Syanna, on the other hand, was definitely *not* writing Book One. When I asked her about her plan for how to start her story, she said that this was a story about the time her new pretend character, Jennifer, had a tooth taken out. Syanna, who had just lost a tooth herself, clearly wanted to get right to describing the anguish of this moment. As she rehearsed her story by touching and telling across pages, I heard her saying just what the characters might say about how much a pulled tooth could hurt. Syanna often had speech bubbles in her writing, which made me think she might be ready to try exciting dialogue as a story lead. "Syanna," I said, "One thing I notice about you as a writer is how often your stories have speech bubbles in them, and how you make the characters talk. You make sure your characters come alive that way, and that's great. But that got me thinking that you could bring that same work to the beginning of the story. Sometimes writers try leads—that's the very first part of the story—that start with dialogue. When they do this, they make the dialogue very exciting, to really put the reader smack into the middle of the story. If you were going to try that, what might it sound like? Give it a go and then I can give you some tips."

This technique, of getting a writer started, and then giving him or her a tip based on data in hand, can help you calibrate your instruction. Syanna, for instance, immediately launched her story with "I do not want the dentist to take out my teeth!" Seeing that she grasped the exciting aspect of such dialogue, and that she indeed knew how to launch her reader into the heart of the story, I gave her a tip about how writers often

explain *why* characters say the things they do or feel the way they do. "She was crying because she did not want the dentist to take out her teeth," Syanna was writing as I left her. I hoped she would try various leads to her stories now, and mostly, I wanted her to begin to take her authorial choices more seriously.

FIG. 11–2   Syanna's fiction story echoes events in her own life, a pattern you'll notice often among your young realistic fiction authors, and one that gives their writing great authenticity.

Taking Just-Right Paper Choices More Seriously

Introduce the notion that writers often move right to writing many sentences, which will change their paper choice.

"Writers, way to go starting your new realistic fiction series! Before we do anything else, tell your partner a few things you did to get started writing a new series. Point to your work to show what you did.

"I imagined a pretend character, and then I thought of calling him up and asking him questions," Robert called out.

Miles told his partner, "I told my story across my fingers, stretching the trouble out."

I gathered their attention. "Eyes on me, please. Nice work, writers. You don't need anyone to start your engine! I was especially pleased to see you not just starting a story, but trying to do your best writing. I love that you were thinking about introducing your character, and making the story realistic. I love that some of you were already working on spelling! I love that you were rehearsing to stretch out the trouble in your story. I can tell that this next series is going to be even better than your first.

"As you become stronger as writers, you might need different paper. It could be you need booklets with more pages. It could be that you need paper with more lines. It could be . . . that you have to make your own booklets now. For instance, Alejandra and I noticed she didn't really need to make so many sketches. So, I showed her this paper with a smaller picture box so there would be room for more lines and more sentences. Now she can write more on each page. Thumbs up if you think you may need paper like this too!"

I waited until a lot of thumbs were up. "Wow! Lots of you. Okay. I will stock the writing center with this kind of paper.

"Wait, there is more. I noticed some of you didn't bother to put a picture on each page. So you might choose paper with all lines and no picture box so some pages can be all sentences. I know this feels like second-grade work, but I see you are ready to make choices like this. So let's add that paper choice to the writing center as well! Don't worry. We will also keep plain blank paper in case you want a full-page picture and our picture box and lined paper too.

"The important thing is that you don't just reach for paper, you think about what paper will help you get a lot of writing done. That might even mean that you make your own booklet, with the paper you need as a writer."

Writers "Show, Not Tell" by Focusing on Tiny Realistic Details

IN THIS SESSION, you'll teach students that fiction writers add tiny, realistic details to their stories—they show, not tell—to help their readers picture the story in their minds.

GETTING READY

✔ The mentor text you have been using. We use *Henry and Mudge and the Happy Cat*. You'll want to have read that story a few times prior to this lesson. (see Connection)

✔ A new character you plan to use in your next series and a story about that character to demonstrate how to show, not tell. We use Sam. (see Teaching)

✔ A new shared class character and story for kids to practice adding details and showing, not telling, during the active engagement. Our new shared class character is Joe. (see Active Engagement)

✔ Chart paper with large picture boxes and lines, to draft a new class story (see Active Engagement)

✔ Cynthia Rylant's *Puppy Mudge*, or another lower-level text, to work with struggling writers during the conferring

COMMON CORE STATE STANDARDS: W.1.3, W.1.5, W.2.3, RL.1.1, RL.1.3, RL.1.4, RL.1.7, SL.1.1, SL.1.4, L.1.1, L.1.2, L.1.5, L.1.6

THIS SESSION BUILDS ON THE LAST ONE, in which children studied the "realistic" in realistic fiction. In that minilesson, children studied what authors do to make their story feel realistic and familiar. The aim of that lesson was overarching—to help children leave aside the aliens, talking animals, and spaceships in favor of realistic characters and places. Now they'll have the opportunity to see how authors pile up small details to help their readers picture the story in their minds.

Now is when you'll see your mentor text really become an extra teacher in the room. We return to *Henry and Mudge and the Happy Cat*. This chapter book does some lovely work with realistic details in both the words and the pictures, making it accessible for readers and writers at different levels. Whether you use this story or another, you'll want to choose a story your children love and know well. That way, your writers can really zoom in on the details, rather than listening for plot—and you can zoom in just on specific parts of the story for your lesson. For instance, in *Henry and Mudge and the Happy Cat*, Cynthia Rylant is particularly effective with her small, realistic details about animals. Mudge and the cat act like real dogs and cats, with all their charming and annoying habits. By piling up details, Cynthia Rylant helps the reader picture the shabby cat and the clumsy dog. She shows rather than tells.

Sometimes, it's helpful to picture what the writing might have sounded like if the author was *not* showing but telling, and what process a writer might go through to show. For instance, when writers tell, they write, "Sam's room was messy." When they show, they might write, "Sam's room had socks strewn about, dirty clothes under the bed, Legos all over the floor, and dust balls in every corner." To do this "showing" work in realistic fiction, writers call on what they readily know about messes. They picture it in their minds and they zoom in on those specific, realistic details such as socks and Legos. That's the same work you want to help children do.

To help them practice this strategy, you'll start with a minilesson that focuses on realistic details about a character or an object. Then later, the mid-workshop teaching and share carry this practice to places and feelings. You could, of course, do all three at once. We've found, though, that when you really want children to follow you, and do what you do with a high-leverage writing move, it's best to be very clear and to do one thing at a time. Showing, not telling, by adding realistic details is a high-leverage writing move.

"When you really want children to follow you, and do what you do with a high-leverage writing move, such as showing, not telling, it's best to be very clear and to do one thing at a time."

Because the teaching and active engagement are fairly heavy-handed, with a "do what I do," kind of feel, you'll notice that the mid-workshop and share highlight how students can adapt and invent their own strategies for continuing this work.

There is one tip we'd like to share with you about "show, not tell." The first stage of accomplishing this craft move is often telling. That is, before a writer can really show how a character looks when she is sad, that writer often needs to tell, "Georgia was sad." So mark the telling as an important sign of readiness for showing. With this in mind, you'll do some telling first, and then move to showing, so that your students can follow in your footsteps.

Writers "Show, Not Tell" by Focusing on Tiny Realistic Details

CONNECTION

Recall the work students did yesterday on studying the realistic details in their mentor text, and build a connection to how those details help writers show, not tell, in their writing.

"Writers, recently we were studying all the parts of *Henry and Mudge and the Happy Cat* and how they felt so realistic." I held the book up again and opened to some favorite pages. "Remember Henry and his Dad and Mudge all squeezed on the couch watching TV? And the barking dog and licking cat? Or when Henry had to go cry a little and take a nap when the policeman came for Dave?

"All those details showed us that this was a real home, with a real boy in it, who feels really sad when he has to give up the cat. Cynthia Rylant didn't just tell us there was a real boy, a real cat, and real emotions. She showed us."

I put the book down. "Writers, you can do this work too. We've talked before about how to show, not tell. Well, that's just what Cynthia Rylant did, isn't it? She added tiny, realistic details to show her reader what happened in her story."

Chances are that your writers have heard "show, don't tell," since they began writing. It's important to add "one way to do this is...." After all, if they knew how to show, not tell, they would be doing it already!

❖ **Name the teaching point.**

"Today I want to teach you that writers *show* their readers what is happening in their story. One way writers do this is by picturing their story, and then adding lots of the realistic, exact details they are picturing to their writing. This way, readers can picture it too."

TEACHING

Establish a new character for your next series. Then explain that your goal as a writer is to show your reader what you picture in your mind. Demonstrate how by first naming what you want to show, or telling it.

"Writers, since you all got started working on a new series yesterday, I decided I would start a new series too. I've started writing my next series about a character named Sam. In my first book, Sam met a dog.

You may have noticed that we've kept our model stories in the past tense. That's to simplify the verb tense choices. Be deliberate with your tenses.

"To get started today, I'm going to really try to picture the scene where Sam met the dog, and *show* my reader some details about the characters. I want to zoom in on the character of the dog. Let's see. I have this one part, right at the beginning, where Sam met the dog and was afraid of it. But in my mind, this is funny, because I imagine this dog was actually kind of small and cute. Let's see. Let me tell this first. If I tell it, I'd say, 'The dog was cute.'"

Recall how the mentor text used details to show things vividly, and revise your own line from your story, where you told, with similar details.

"But wait, that's not what Cynthia Rylant does." I opened the page to the description of the shabby cat. "When we meet the cat, she doesn't just *tell* us that it was shabby. She *shows* us. She writes, 'It had a saggy belly, skinny legs, and fur that looked like mashed prunes.' Mashed prunes! I'm not sure I've ever eaten those but they sound gross! Cynthia Rylant really wanted us to picture how shabby the cat was. She uses a lot of tiny details, like the saggy belly, skinny legs, and fur like prunes. I bet she's seen a cat like that.

"So, instead of writing, 'The dog was cute,' maybe I can show too. Hmm. First, I'll picture a cute dog in my mind." I closed my eyes. "I'm picturing that . . . the dog had floppy ears . . . a wagging tail . . . and a happy grin." I opened my eyes. "That would work, right? Now you can really picture a cute, friendly dog. Did you see how I pictured in my mind what a real dog would look like, and then I described some of those real details?"

ACTIVE ENGAGEMENT

Invite your students to coauthor a new shared class character and story. Focus on showing the reader realistic details, starting with something familiar that the children will be able to envision easily.

"Writers, let's try this together. First we need to come up with a new class character and some new trouble for that character." After some quick discussion and compromise, we decided to write about Joe, who had a new fancy bike that got ruined in an accident.

I flipped the chart open to a few picture boxes and quickly sketched a picture of Joe and his bike to get us started. "I've sketched a picture to start our story. In the first picture, Joe had a new bike. So let's tell first. 'Joe had a new bike. The bike was fancy.' Now let's try showing that the new bike was fancy. 'The bike was shiny red. It . . . '" I paused. "Hmm, let's close our eyes for a second. When you're picturing a fancy red bike, I mean when you can really see it in your mind, give a thumbs up." I gave a moment of silence until thumbs were up. "Okay, with that picture in your mind, turn and tell your partner, quickly, what details we should write to show the bike is fancy." I wrote on the chart paper, under the sketch, "Joe had a new bike. The bike was fancy."

They turned and talked. I listened in, and then called them back.

Summarize the details students shared. You might label some of the details on your story sketch so you can write it up later as a model.

"Let's hear some of the details we can write to show the bike was fancy. What should we add?"

Robert said, "The bike had a bell *and* a horn."

Miles added, "And it had a special light."

Annabel tucked in, "The seat was shiny black.'"

As they said these details, I jotted "bell, horn, light, and shiny black seat," on the sketch. Then I moved my finger across the page as if I were actually writing the words. "Yes, let's try that. 'Joe had a new bike. The bike was fancy. The bike had a bell, and a horn, and a special light, and a shiny black seat.' That really does show how fancy this bike was."

Skip ahead to the second picture box on your chart paper and coauthor details for the next part of your story.

"That was great, writers. Now, let's skip ahead in the story. In that part, Joe had an accident with his new bike. Maybe he rode it in the rain and wiped out, or maybe he hit a rock or something. We can work on stretching the trouble part out later. For now, let's try adding details that show how after the accident, Joe's bike was *not* fancy anymore! In fact, let's show that it was wrecked! Maybe it will start with 'Joe looked at his bike. The bike was . . .' " I closed my eyes. "Are you picturing it? Let's not just tell our readers it's wrecked, let's show them. Close your eyes. Are you picturing a bike that is destroyed? Put a thumb up when you're picturing a wrecked bike." I peeked, looking for thumbs to go up. "Quick, turn and tell your partner how to show Joe's bike is wrecked."

Again, listen in and then summarize the details. Add them to your sketch if you have time, and write-in-the-air what the full sentences would sound like.

I listened in for a bit, then said, "Wow, I heard some truly awful details! This poor bike. Joe is going to be very sad. Okay, let's add what you said. This time I'm going to sum up what a lot of you said. You mentioned smashed parts and ripped parts and parts that were gone. It could go . . . 'Joe looked at his bike. The bike was broken and muddy. The horn was gone. The bell was smashed. The seat was ripped. One wheel was . . . *gone*!'" As I spoke, slowly, I created a quick sketch, capturing our thinking with some labels on the page.

"Yes! Now both parts of this story really show the bike and how different it was before and after the accident. First, you pictured what a fancy new bike would look like. That helped you add a lot of fancy details. Then, you pictured what a wrecked bike would look like. That helped you add a lot of awful details."

This lesson has a double active engagement for repeated practice and to demonstrate contrasting details.

LINK

Send students off while they are excited about this new skill and have a sense of what it sounds like. Ensure that they know they can put this skill to work at any point of the writing process.

"Writers, as you go off, remember that the tiniest details will make a difference. Like the bell that was new, and then got smashed. You'll want to go do this work in your own stories. Whether you are sketching or telling a new story or writing or revising one from yesterday, you can picture the scene in your mind, then show your reader the tiny, realistic details to bring every little part of your story to life. Off you go."

Helping Writers Show, Not Tell Using Leveled Texts

WHILE MANY OF YOUR WRITERS will follow Cynthia Rylant's lead to "show, not tell" quite easily, you may have others who struggle with adding this kind of descriptive detail to their writing. If you do have some of these writers in your class, you may decide to pull them together and use a mentor text that matches more closely what they might actually do. Luckily, Cynthia Rylant has a series called Puppy Mudge. It is a lower-level version of Henry and Mudge that is perfect for studying craft that is more appropriate for these writers. One of the differences of this lower-level Mudge story is that more of the details are shown in the pictures.

I decided to pull a small group together and coach them to add details to their pictures first to show, not tell. Having had success before with these writers when they had a chance to act out parts of their stories, I thought I could help them practice a process of showing with their bodies first, then adding details to their pictures, and then adding some of those details in words.

I gathered a group of students to the meeting area, along with their writing folders and pens. I began by saying, "Writers, look what I found!" I held up the book *Puppy Mudge*. "Cynthia Rylant has a book about Mudge as a puppy. Isn't he cute?! Let's look closely at some of the pictures without reading the words, to see if we can say what is happening."

Together we looked at a picture of Mudge running after a cat. I then said, "See if you can say a lot about what you see, what is happening, and how the characters look and feel."

Immediately kids began calling out, "Mudge is running."

"A cat is running too."

"Maybe they are playing chase?"

"Mudge likes cats. He looks like he is having fun."

"Wow, you got all of that and we didn't even read the words yet. You are such strong readers. Nice work!"

MID-WORKSHOP TEACHING
Writers Show, Not Tell How a Character Is Feeling

"Writers, I want to give you a tip. Remember in *Henry and Mudge and the Happy Cat* how Cynthia Rylant showed us Henry was *sad* by writing that Henry had to cry a little and take a nap? She didn't just *show* actions or thoughts, she also *showed* us how her character was feeling. Well, that got me thinking. In my story about Sam, Sam is really scared at the beginning of the story, remember? I bet I can *show* my reader that, just like Cynthia Rylant does. If I picture in my mind how Sam might look scared, I can probably add more sentences to my story." I closed my eyes and put my hands to my head to demonstrate picturing how Sam might look scared. "Hmm . . . I might write, 'Sam's hands were shaking and he started to sweat.' See how I did that, writers? I didn't just tell the reader that Sam was scared. I showed it—with real details. How many of you have started to shake or sweat when you were scared?

"I know you're going to want to do this too when you find a part of your story where someone feels a strong feeling. Really picture in your mind what that feeling might look like, and show it to your reader with realistic, exact details. Think about what you do when you have that feeling!"

Next, I invited children to find the story that they were working on, and to choose a part to work on "show, not tell." First, I had them point to the part of the story, especially the sketch they had made. Then, I had them tell their partner what was happening. Next I had them close their eyes, and try to really picture the scene in their mind. Then I invited them to get out of their seats, and act out what was happening. Soon some were buzzing like bees, climbing trees, falling off swings. In the midst of this merriment I "froze" them. "Remember this moment," I said. "Remember the sound of the bee buzzing, the feel of the bark as you climbed the tree, how hard the ground was when you fell off the swing. Picture, right now, what you are hearing, feeling, every detail . . . now, quickly, add some of those details and labels to your picture. See if you can each capture three new details."

The kids held their poses for a moment, then sat and began adding in details to their pictures. I bounced around, coaching them by saying, "Show me how he feels. Okay, now make your character look like that." Or "Where is he? What can you add to your picture so the reader will know?" As kids responded I simply said, "Okay, add that in!" This kept the pacing going and the enthusiasm up.

We then shared a few examples of the work they did. In Sahadat's story, a boy named Ben fell off his bike riding down a hill on his way to the park. So Sahadat drew a picture of the playground in the distance so the reader would know he was headed that way. He also made Ben look like he was lying flat on the ground after he fell, with his mouth open to show the dramatic fall off his bike! He even added pieces of the bike to show that the bike broke (see Figure 12–1).

After sharing a few examples, I reminded the children that their detailed pictures would now help them add words to their stories. With each writer, I had them point to at least one detail that they wanted to add to their text. Then I sent them off to continue writing.

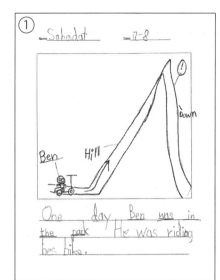

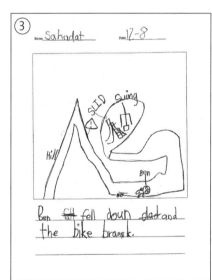

FIG. 12–1   Sahadat's illustrations in which he adds details to enhance the realism and drama of his story

Showing Realistic Settings

Describe how writers include realistic details for new settings by remembering places they have been that are similar to places in their stories.

"Writers, we're going to stay in our writing spots for our share today. A few of you have done some work that will help all of us. Annabel and her partner were trying to figure out how to show, not tell about the place—or setting—of Annabel's story. In the story, her character goes into a dark attic. An attic is a room at the top of a house, where people store stuff they don't use, like old boxes of toys or winter coats. Now, Annabel said she's never been in an attic because she doesn't have an attic! And then Annabel's partner, Nora, came up with this great strategy. She figured out that even though neither of them have been in an attic, they could picture other creepy places they've been in, and it turns out Nora has a creepy basement storage area! So they thought about that place and added all these details that sound so real and creepy. Listen to these sentences for how they showed the attic was creepy."

> The attic was creepy. It had spiders, and cobwebs, and dark corners. It had dark places and no windows. CREEPY!

"Isn't that a helpful strategy, writers? I love the way they figured out their own strategy when things got hard. You might also want to do what Annabel and Nora did in your own stories. Think of *real* places that are *like* places in your story, when you want to show what the place—or setting—is like in your story!"

Session 13

Fiction Writers Include Chapters

Writing a Beginning, Middle, and End

S OMETIMES WHEN YOU TEACH CHILDREN, you disguise what you are really teaching with a spin to increase engagement. Today's session has some of this spin. It will sound to your children as if they are pleasing their readers by introducing chapters. But really, they're also working on structure and telling a story across a sequence of organized small moments.

In the first part of the unit, your children stretched out their stories by thinking about getting their character into trouble, and then getting their character out of trouble. This session will add to that work of stretching out stories. Thinking of beginnings, middles, and endings is another way to work on telling a story bit by bit, stretching out each part. There is another reason to focus on beginning, middles, and endings, though, and that is because it helps young writers develop a sense of sequence—of story structure. Sometimes when you read children's writing, there is a startling moment when you wonder if they are followers of the French filmmaker Jean-Luc Godard, who believed that "every story should have a beginning, middle, and end—just not in that order." You find yourself reading and rereading, asking, "What, exactly, is happening here?"

These gaps can especially happen when children begin to stretch their stories over more than one day of writing. Day one, the frog dies. Day two, he is alive again. In between those scenes of a story, nothing. In between those scenes in a writer's life, though, many things happened, and the writer returned with a different story in mind, or perhaps, no recollection of the prior day's effort.

One of the habits that you may want to instill in your young writers, then, is the habit of rereading their writing. Just as children who read longer books begin to need bookmarks, and strategies for retelling their stories before they read again, children who write longer stories need strategies for reminding themselves what they were writing.

This session offers up the emphasis on beginnings, middles, and endings through the lens of introducing chapters in a story. You may, at this point, want to consider expanding the size of your students' booklets, or have children begin to make their own booklets, adding pages in as needed. That magic number of five may be too small a container now

IN THIS SESSION, you'll teach students that fiction writers divide their stories into chapters and they stretch out each chapter so that they have a beginning, a middle, and an ending for their stories.

GETTING READY

- Fully stocked writing center, perhaps including some booklets that are six and seven pages each, and extra paper and tape for students to add pages to their booklets as needed.

- Your mentor text, in this case, *Henry and Mudge and the Happy Cat* (see Connection)

- A new fiction story that has a clear beginning, middle, and end for you to demonstrate making chapters. This should use the same character you introduced in Session 12. We use Sam. (see Teaching)

- A chart with Chapters One, Two, Three written on it in a table of contents format, with room for you to add titles for each (see Teaching)

- Chart paper and markers, for the active engagement

- Narrative Writing Checklists, Grades 1 and 2 (see Share)

- The goals students set for themselves (on note cards) in Session 5, for the share

- Post-its and note cards for the share

COMMON CORE STATE STANDARDS: W.1.3, W.1.5, W.2.3, RL.1.1, RL.1.3, RL.2.5, SL.1.1, L.1.1, L.1.2

for writers who are writing in chapters. You might, therefore, put together some booklets of six to seven pages. Or you might encourage children to tape their pages together as they plan, using the "touch and tell" strategy to figure out how many pages they'll need for their chapters.

"Thinking of beginnings, middles, and endings is another way to work on telling a story bit by bit, stretching out each part."

Today you will look at chapters, returning to your mentor text—perhaps *Henry and Mudge and the Happy Cat*—to see how the chapters work as the beginning, middle, and end of the book, and then trying out chapters in your demonstration text before children give it a go with their own stories.

Fiction Writers Include Chapters

Writing a Beginning, Middle, and End

CONNECTION

Gather children and show them how your mentor text is broken into chapters. Act as if this is something you just realized, and make a big deal of it.

"Series authors, come close. I want to show you something I noticed as I was reading our favorite mentor text, *Henry and Mudge and the Happy Cat*. I noticed that Cynthia Rylant divides her story into chapters. Look." I held the book open to the chapter titles and read them.

Focusing writers' attention on the beginning, middle, and end helps them to develop a sense of story structure, and is a building block for the story tension they'll eventually work on. You may find it helpful to echo this work in reading workshop. If you occasionally have children recall and retell stories, you might have them do it focusing on the beginning, middle, and end, and use similar transition words, such as first, next, then, *and* finally.

Henry and Mudge and the Happy Cat

Chapter One: What Is It?

Chapter Two: A Good Mother

Chapter Three: A Surprise

I put the book down and looked up at the children. "Hmm, what did Cynthia Rylant probably do to come up with chapters? Her chapters went Chapter One, the *beginning*, where Henry gets the cat; Chapter Two, *the middle*, where the cat takes care of Mudge; and Chapter Three, *the ending*, where the owner takes it back. Cynthia Rylant must have thought through what would happen in the story and then made each chapter one part—a beginning, a middle, and an ending.

"Don't you think you could do that too? You could have chapters in your stories! Readers *love* chapters because it helps them get excited for what is coming next in the story." The children nodded enthusiastically.

❖ **Name the teaching point.**

Chapter books still hold allure for your writers. It's not so long ago after all, that many of them were reading books without sections. The glamour of chapters helps excite writers as well as readers.

"Writers, today I want to teach you that fiction writers often divide their story into chapters. One way they do this is to break their story into three parts: the beginning, the middle (or trouble), and the end (or fixing the trouble)."

TEACHING

Set up your demonstration by explaining what happens in the story you are rehearsing.

"Let's give this a try. I'll try it on the story I'm working on right now about Sam. Let's see. In this story, Sam faced another dog. Last time, the dog he faced was cute, and Sam was silly to be afraid. This time, though, the dog was *not* cute, and Sam almost got bitten." I made a fierce face and snapped as I said *bitten*, and the children gasped.

Demonstrate what it looks like to rehearse chapters as parts of a story. Intentionally struggle where you know your students might have difficulty to model how they can revise their thinking.

"Okay, let me try this. Watch how I plan out a beginning, a middle—or the trouble, and an end—or fixing the trouble." I demonstrated planning my chapters across my fingers, unfolding a new finger for each transition word. "In my story, *in the beginning* Sam faced another dog, *in the middle*, the trouble part, he almost got bitten, and *at the end*, the part where the trouble is fixed, he realized he should be more careful.

"Writers, did you see how I divided the main parts of my story into the beginning, then the trouble, and then fixing the trouble? Those could be my chapters. Now, I can think about what will go in each chapter, and make sure it makes sense—that I've got the order right. Let me see . . . "

I pointed to the chart paper, where I had written "Chapters One, Two, and Three," as I rehearsed each chapter.

"So maybe . . . Chapter One: Sam saw a big guard dog. It looked pretty mean. Chapter Two: Sam tried to pat the guard dog through the fence. Chapter Three: The dog tried to bite Sam. No, wait! That doesn't sound like an ending, does it? I have to get my character out of trouble." The children nodded. "I'll add the dog tried to bite Sam into Chapter Two. That means maybe Chapter Three can be . . . Sam saw the 'Beware of Dog' sign and realized how lucky he was!

"Okay, I think that's working. Do you see how I thought through what would happen in my story, and then I tried to divide it into parts—the beginning, the trouble, and the fixing the trouble? Only I got confused for a minute, and my ending wasn't really an ending, so I had to do it again.

"So the first step is to plan out a beginning, middle (the trouble), and end (fixing the trouble) as three chapters. Then the second step is to tell what happens in each chapter."

Demonstrate how writers give titles to chapters based on what happens. This is easy for children, so keep it small.

"One last step writers—you can then write some snappy titles for your chapters. Let me try that. I usually remind myself what happens in the chapter, then try out a title."

You are probably building on work you've done in reading workshop as well as prior narrative writing. The Common Core State Standards for reading ask children to recount stories as a sequence of events, in logical order. If children struggle with this work, here you can reinforce that crucial reading work, in writing workshop.

As you model, it's actually helpful not *to create a perfect sequence the first time. Instead, do what your children often do, then show them how to rethink and improve their sequence of events so it feels more as if there is an ending.*

I muttered about what happened in each chapter again. As I muttered about what happened in Chapter One, I wrote, "The New Dog." Then I retold a little bit more, writing possible titles.

"How exciting. My readers are going to love having chapters, and I think they'll like these snappy titles. They'll look at the titles and think, 'What happens in that chapter? I can't wait to find out!'"

ACTIVE ENGAGEMENT

Recruit writers to give this a try with your shared class story. Tuck in practice with narrative structure by emphasizing the beginning, middle (trouble), and ending (fixing the trouble).

"Let's give you a chance to try this out, writers. Let's try it once together, so I can give you some tips. Ready?

"Okay, let's work with this story about our class character, Joe. Let's imagine Joe forgot to lock his bike outside the store, and it got stolen. Joe almost lied to his dad—he was so scared—but then he told the truth! Okay, let's tell that again. First, Joe took his new bike to the store, with his new lock. At the store, he forgot to lock it. When he came out, the bike was gone! Joe was afraid, but he told the truth.

"Writers, in just a minute, I want you to plan chapters for this story. But first, here's a tip. The first thing you do when you think about chapters is you try telling the story first to yourself, or to your partner, and you try telling it as 'in the beginning, in the middle, and in the ending.' Partner 1, try telling the story to your partner, across your fingers. Partner 2, you can listen for any missing parts and add them in."

The children did this work. Some used words such as *first*, *next*, *then*, and *finally*. I took note of these children so that later I could pull them into advanced small-group work. Then I gathered children's attention.

Invite the children to have a go at snappy chapter titles.

"Okay, you've got this story down. Now let's give a quick try at some snappy chapter titles. Let's try for a chapter that is the beginning of the story, a chapter that is the middle, or the trouble, and a chapter that is the ending, or fixing the trouble. Work with your partner, see what snappy titles you can come up with." The children began to invent avidly. I listened in, noting how they moved from parts to chapters to snappy titles. I jotted a few on a chart.

Sam and the Guard Dog

Chapter one: The New Dog

Chapter Two: A Big Mistake

Chapter Three: Beware Of Dog

Do a quick share of some of the titles, showing students a few different ways the chapters could go, so they have a model on a teaching chart.

"Okay, writers, I think you have this down. Here are a couple of snappy chapter titles I heard." I pointed to the chart.

Joe and The lost bike

Chapter one: Don't forget the lock

Chapter TWO: Oh No! It's GONE

Chapter Three: It's Hard to Tell the Truth

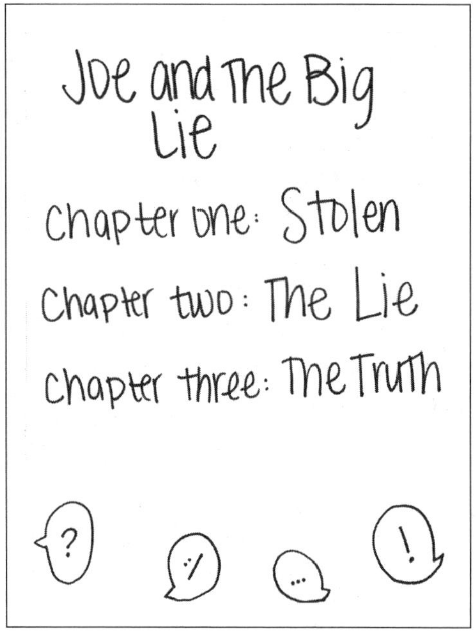

Joe and The Big Lie

Chapter one: Stolen

Chapter two: The Lie

Chapter three: The Truth

I looked up. "Very cool, writers."

LINK

As you send children off, invite them to invent ways to plan and stretch out the parts of their stories into chapters. Tuck in some of what they know how to do to plan and stretch out parts.

"Writers, this work is going to really pay off as you are planning your stories. Writing chapter titles and rehearsing each chapter is a great way to plan a story. So if you start a new story today, or any day, give this a try. One tip, writers, as you stretch out all the parts of your stories, you're writing more, and this means you're often working on stories for more than one day. That means you should start each writing session by rereading what you wrote last time, *then* starting the next part of your story. That way you won't forget a part! Off you go! Your readers are waiting for your next series books!"

Supporting Students with Structure and Elaboration

YOU MAY DECIDE to approach your conferring and small-group work today with a focus on both structure (writing a beginning, middle, and end), and elaboration (writing long about each part of the story). Once kids have a sense for the beginning, middle, and end of their stories, or the introduction, the trouble, and the solution, the next task is to write a lot about each part to stretch out the story. Regardless of what your focus is for individual students or small groups, all your writers will probably need reminders that even though they are focusing on structure, they still need to be doing everything they've been taught about strong narrative writing.

One possible problem you may encounter is that some kids literally take their initial plan of first, then next, and finally and actually write their story just like that. For example, you may see the following: "First Piper went to get ice cream, then she dropped it, next she cried, finally her brother shared his." It is as if they forgot everything they learned about using story language and narrative writing. It suddenly may sound like how-to/procedural-type writing. If you see this you can easily shift it back by teaching leads. You might, for instance, invite kids to think about their opening line or two. You can remind them of the "One day . . ." opening and then look at a few books to see how other writers begin their texts to get more ideas. Some writers start with the setting and time of day or with someone speaking. This will quickly get your students back to story language.

On the other hand, you may see kids busy writing in an organized way with a clear beginning, middle, and end complete with chapter titles and story language. So your focus for them may be to teach, coach, or remind them of ways to add more. You can show these writers that each part of their stories can be filled with action, dialogue, characters' thoughts, feelings, and the setting.

In addition, you may decide to pull a group and revisit the work you taught on endings. You can have kids unstaple their booklets and add some new and improved revised pages to the end. Hopefully, by now they have moved on from "and then I went home" as their last page. Whether they are still doing this or not, you will likely find kids who need help ending their stories.

MID-WORKSHOP TEACHING
Adding Chapters to Stories We've Already Written

"Writers, I want to point out something that I saw Annabel doing in her writing that I think many of you might want to try out too. Annabel had already written a story about her character, Violet, and how she lived in the country and found a newborn puppy. Violet decided to go back into that story and write chapter titles at the top of her pages. She decided that Chapter One should be about finding the puppy, and that Chapter Two should be about how Violet takes the puppy home and tries to convince her mom to let her keep it. I can't wait to see what happens at the end in Chapter Three! Will her mom let her keep the puppy? (See Figure 13–1.)

"Some of you may already be trying this in your writing, too, going back into stories you've already written and seeing if you can divide it into chapters. You might see if you have a beginning about your character, a middle with some trouble, and an ending where you get your character out of trouble. Going back to see if you have chapters in your earlier stories might give you ideas for how to revise those stories too. Thanks for sharing that great strategy, Annabel!"

(continues)

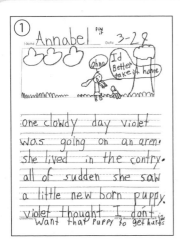

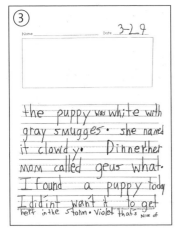

FIG. 13–1 Annabel stretches out her story so that the beginning introduces the character, and the middle develops the trouble.

Ch 1–Find it

Page 1: One cloudy day Violet was going on an errand. She lived in the county. All of a sudden she saw a little new born puppy. Violet thought I don't want that puppy to get hurt.

Ch 2–Get it Comfy

Page 2: She took the puppy into her room. Here I'll put you in a box and give you my small blanket.

Page 3: The puppy was white with gray smudges. She named it Clowdy. Dinner! Her mom called. Guess what? I found a puppy today. I didn't want it to get hurt in the storm.

Page 4: You tried to save a puppy. But me and your father don't want a dog. But she is s-o-o-o cute. You can keep her until her mom comes. okay mom. Violet please go to your room and get your pajamas.

Page 5: Violet thought I really want to keep the puppy. How will I get mom to like dogs? Go to bed Violet her mom called.

Self-Assessment and Goal Setting

Set children's sights on the second-grade goals they should be working toward by now, using the Narrative Writing Checklist.

After calling students to the rug with their folders, I said, "Writers, many of you have met your goals—the ones you set when you looked at the Narrative Writing Checklist over a week ago. Right now—find the Post-its that had your goals on them as writers." I waited for this to happen, leaning in to help some students find their materials in their folders. "Now, writers—prove it. Find some stories in your folder that prove you met your goals." I waited a moment. "Show your partner where, specifically, you did some writing that shows you met your goals as a writer."

After a moment, I paused the children. "Pat yourself on the back, writers!" I waited for them to congratulate themselves. Then I motioned for their attention. In a suspenseful voice I asked, "Do you know what this means, writers?" I paused dramatically. "This means, famous series authors, you have proven yourself worthy to tackle . . . the second-grade side of the checklist!

"Let's take a look again at this super-duper second-grade Narrative Writing Checklist and see which of these things you might try as a writer. As we read through the list, be thinking, 'Which of these do I want to do next as a writer?'" I read through the list, commenting after some of the items, saying things like, "This one you are all ready to do!" or "Oh my gosh, I think you already do this! Give yourself a pat on the back if you've done this already."

Narrative Writing Checklist

	Grade 1	NOT YET	STARTING TO	YES!	Grade 2	NOT YET	STARTING TO	YES!
	Structure				**Structure**			
Overall	I wrote about when I did something.	☐	☐	☐	I wrote about *one time* when I did something.	☐	☐	☐
Lead	I tried to make a beginning for my story.	☐	☐	☐	I thought about how to write a good beginning and chose a way to start my story. I chose the action, talk, or setting that would make a good beginning.	☐	☐	☐
Transitions	I put my pages in order. I used words such as *and* and *then, so*.	☐	☐	☐	I told the story in order by using words such as *when, then*, and *after*.	☐	☐	☐
Ending	I found a way to end my story.	☐	☐	☐	I chose the action, talk, or feeling that would make a good ending.	☐	☐	☐
Organization	I wrote my story across three or more pages.	☐	☐	☐	I wrote a lot of lines on a page and wrote across a lot of pages.	☐	☐	☐
	Development				**Development**			
Elaboration	I put the picture from my mind onto the page. I had details in pictures and words.	☐	☐	☐	I tried to bring my characters to life with details, talk, and actions.	☐	☐	☐
Craft	I used labels and words to give details.	☐	☐	☐	I chose strong words that would help readers picture my story.	☐	☐	☐
	Language Conventions				**Language Conventions**			
Spelling	I used all I knew about words and chunks of words (*at, op, it*, etc.) to help me spell.	☐	☐	☐	To spell a word, I used what I knew about spelling patterns (*tion, er, ly*, etc.).	☐	☐	☐
	I spelled all the word wall words right and used the word wall to help me spell other words.	☐	☐	☐	I spelled all of the word wall words correctly and used the word wall to help me figure out how to spell other words.	☐	☐	☐

Channel children to look for one item from the second-grade side of the checklist to see if they are doing it across all the books they've written so far in their series.

"Now, writers, if you think you are already doing one of these things, the important part is that you do it in more than one book in your series. Remember, writers don't just do something once or do it *sometimes* or in *some* books. They try it out in all their writing. Right now, go through your books and see how many times you did that one thing. If you notice some spots where you can add it, mark it with a Post-it so you can go back to it later."

Rally students to look for another item on the checklist that can be a new goal to work toward.

"Writers, now, quick as a wink, look for a new goal you can tackle in your writing. Pick something out—and then find a place in your books where you could do this work. Remember to look at not just the book you worked on today, but *all* the fiction books in your series. You might even look at the stories you wrote for your first series. If you finish with one item, move on to another item on the list and set another goal! Find some places where you could add new writing, and put a Post-it there to remind yourself—then you can tackle this goal right away!"

End by having students work toward a new goal for themselves.

"Writers, great work at looking through your writing for just one goal—one item on the list—at a time. Now, we know that when writers set goals, they work on them right away. So right now, right here, find a Post-it for where you wanted to add new writing. Think of this new goal you have. And give it your best shot."

Patterns Help Writers Elaborate

N OT LONG AGO YOUR YOUNG WRITERS were reading pattern books. Patterns weave through the books children learn to read with. These patterns range from simple repetitions such as "the boat is red, the car is red, the bike is red, the bus is yellow," to the narrative patterns that run through stories like Mr. Putter and Tabby, where these friends set out each time on an adventure, and whether it is painting the porch or baking a cake, something goes awry in the middle, and all is well by the end.

Patterns create structure; patterns create rhythm; patterns delight the reader. There is something lyrical and pleasing about patterns, perhaps in the way they reveal themselves to the reader so easily. Who hasn't sung the chorus to a song over and over, long after you've forgotten the rest of the lyrics?

This session investigates Cynthia Rylant's use of patterns in *Henry and Mudge and the Happy Cat*, though you may choose a different mentor text. Rylant uses a lot of patterns; she uses them to stretch out parts and to create lovely rhythms. After investigating patterns in her text, you'll create another pattern in your demonstration, which will be modeled exactly on the language of the mentor text—this is a form of mimetic writing that can be very effective. Your children will also have a chance to do this work themselves, using your shared class series. There's a reason for this emphasis on repetition, immediate practice, and a "do it *just like* she did" technique. For each of these patterns, you'll find that if you repeat the same pattern that the mentor text uses, exactly, kids will pick up the language and structure and mimic it. You'll notice that in the link to this lesson, therefore, you'll invite students to give this strategy a try right away, whereas usually you list all the choices they have about what they could do during work time. This is because with this kind of mimetic writing, while the sounds are still fresh in their minds, children will often mimic the sentence structure and language of their mentor and intuitively raise the level of their writing, much the same way apprentices in the medieval period copied the work of master craftsmen.

IN THIS SESSION, you'll teach students that writers use patterns to elaborate.

GETTING READY

✔ Mentor text, *Henry and Mudge and the Happy Cat*, to demonstrate patterns

✔ Prewritten chart that lists the patterns found in the mentor text (see Teaching)

✔ The demonstration story you wrote chapters for yesterday (using your new series character), and some ideas for how to include a pattern in that story (see Teaching)

✔ Chart paper and markers, to write your demonstration text and to record the shared class story (see Teaching and Active Engagement)

✔ Shared class story (same one used during yesterday's minilesson) for kids to practice adding a pattern during the active engagement. We reference the second class character, Joe, and how he lied about locking his bike.

✔ Students' books from independent reading time and Post-its (see Share)

COMMON CORE STATE STANDARDS: W.1.3, W.1.5, W.1.7, W.1.8, W.2.3, RL.1.1, RL.1.4, SL.1.1, SL.1.2, L.1.1, L.1.2

Patterns Help Writers Elaborate

CONNECTION

Create a sense of excitement around the patterns you've noticed in your mentor text, and read aloud a few examples.

"Writers, I was rereading *Henry and Mudge and the Happy Cat* again! I know, I just can't get enough of this book. I noticed that Cynthia Rylant does the coolest thing. She puts all these patterns into her story. Listen."

I picked up the book. "This is the part where the shabby cat moves in. It says, 'It loved three things about Henry's house. It loved the towel closet. It loved the bathtub. And it loved Mudge.' Do you hear the pattern? It's like those pattern books you used to read. 'It loved the towel closet. It loved the bathtub. And it loved Mudge.' I'm going to read you another little part. Put your thumb in the air when you hear a pattern. Here's a hint. It will have three things in it again."

I waited until all eyes were on me, then read, "'It washed Mudge all the time. It washed Mudge's ears. It washed Mudge's eyes.'" Thumbs began to wave in the air. "'It even washed Mudge's dirty feet.'" Now all the thumbs were waving, and I heard whispers of "Three!"

Invite children to share a ritual, such as thumbs up when they hear a pattern.

"Wait!" I said excitedly, turning the page. "Listen to this! Thumbs up if you hear another pattern. 'The cat also made Mudge use good manners. Mudge had to wait his turn at the water dish. Mudge had to share his dog toys. Mudge even had to share his crackers.'" Thumbs were waving wildly. "Three again!" the children whispered.

"I think we can try this too, writers. We'll just copy what Cynthia Rylant does. It seems as if Cynthia Rylant uses patterns of three details to stretch out parts of her story. The cat doesn't just love Henry's house. It loves three things about the house. The towels, the bathtub, and Mudge. The cat doesn't just wash Mudge. It washes three parts of Mudge! His ears, his eyes, his dirty feet! There is something magical about a pattern of three."

❧ Name the teaching point.

"Writers, today I want to teach you that famous writers like Cynthia Rylant play with patterns to stretch out parts of their stories. One way they do that is to work in three details, or three examples, when describing something."

You may decide to use a different mentor text than Henry and Mudge and the Happy Cat. *There are lots of options to choose from, as patterns can be found in many of the books your students are reading. Some great examples of books with patterns include the Poppleton series and the Mr. Putter and Tabby series, though your class may have their own favorites.*

You might notice that we conflate "play with" and "work in" here, inviting children to play with language in a part of their story. When children play, they often work hard—at blocks, at bicycling, at pretend games, sports, all their endeavors where they push themselves. Conflating play and work emphasizes the way writers push themselves to try things again and again.

TEACHING

Invite students to watch you try to write like your mentor text, with patterns of three details.

"Let's give this a try. I'm so excited. Trying something in my writing that someone famous like Cynthia Rylant does makes *me* feel like a famous writer. Okay, I'm going to try to elaborate—or stretch out—a part in my latest story about Sam, by adding in three details. Let's see. I was writing the part of the story where Sam's dad warned him to lock his bike, only Sam still left it unlocked outside a store. So, first I'll figure out the part I want to elaborate, or stretch out. I think I'll work with the part where Sam was warned to lock his bike. Let me see how Cynthia Rylant did this."

Model your language exactly on your mentor text so it's easy for kids to follow what you're doing and see the pattern.

I gestured to the chart, where I had written Cynthia Rylant's patterns.

Patterns in <u>Henry and Mudge and the Happy Cat</u>

It loved three things about Henry's house.
- ✓ It loved the towel closet.
- ✓ It loved the bathtub.
- ✓ And it loved Mudge.

It washed Mudge all the time.
- ✓ It washed Mudge's ears.
- ✓ It washed Mudge's eyes.
- ✓ It even washed Mudge's dirty feet.

"Writers, I notice that when Cynthia Rylant elaborates with a pattern in her story, she adds three details about a feeling or an action. I think I'll try elaborating a feeling. So, my last story in my new series, about Sam, was about when he tried to pet the wrong dog! Remember, it's that guard dog, and there was a sign that said 'Beware of dog,' but Sam didn't read it, and he stuck his fingers through the fence? My feeling will be where Sam was afraid of the dog. Hmm . . . " I closed my eyes as I spoke, thinking and "playing" aloud. "Maybe . . . Sam was afraid of the dog. He was afraid it would growl. He was afraid it would snap. He was afraid it would bark . . . that could work. Or maybe . . . Sam was afraid . . . the dog would bite him, the dog would scratch him, and the dog would hurt him. Let me try one more. So. . . . " This time as I said the words aloud, I nodded as if I liked the pattern and I jotted as I spoke.

Sam was afraid of three parts of the dog.
He was afraid of its teeth.
He was afraid of its claws.
He was even afraid of its tail.

Sam was afraid of three parts of the dog.

He was afraid of its teeth.
He was afraid of its claws.
He was afraid of its tail.

"I noticed that Cynthia Rylant did that in her writing, 'It *even* washed . . . '" I pointed to that part in the third bullet, "so I tried that too."

I leaned back. "What do you think? Is it like Cynthia Rylant? Shall I keep it?" I was answered with emphatic nods. "Okay then, I'll get some flaps out and add this in! I'm so excited about stretching out part of *my* story with a pattern."

ACTIVE ENGAGEMENT

Invite students to give this a try, using the class story from your new series. Give the students a starter sentence.

"Writers, this is so cool. Let's give you a chance to try this. Let's see, why don't you try it in our shared class story first, so you can make that one better, and then you can play with a pattern in your own writing. So, the last story in our new series, about Joe, was about when he lied to his dad about locking his bike! Remember, his dad warned him but Joe didn't listen, and his bike got stolen? Let's see. How about if you try creating a pattern of three details? I'll give you the main sentence, and you and your partner can work together to create a pattern of three off of this one sentence. Then if you want to do another one, go to it. How about. . . ? "

I paused, as if thinking, then wrote on the chart paper, and said, "Joe had been warned three times." Then I looked up. "I bet you can think of three details of ways he'd been warned, can't you! Give it a try with your partner. I'll listen in. Heck, try it more than once if you want. It's really fun."

As the children invent, listen in to capture their words. Jot down examples to share.

"Writers, I love it! I'm loving the patterns . . . I'm loving the way you elaborated a part . . . I'm loving the rhythm!" I laughed, as some of them put their thumbs in the air when they heard three things again. I could tell we'd be getting a lot of thumbs up during read-aloud from now on. "Let me say back some of your ideas." I gestured toward the chart I had recorded their ideas on.

Joe had been warned three times.	**Joe had been warned three times.**
His mother warned him.	His father told him once.
His father warned him.	His father told him twice.
Even his little sister warned him!	His father told him three times to lock his bike!

Really celebrate students' inventiveness and experimentation. Have fun with patterns in your own language.

"Love it, love it, love it!" More thumbs in the air. "There really is something magical about stretching out an action or feeling with three details. I love seeing your patterns. And I love how you invented all these great details, which is something we've been working on. I bet you'd like to shake hands with Cynthia Rylant right now, writers. She is really teaching you a lot of cool stuff."

LINK

Rally students to try a pattern in one of their own stories while this work is fresh.

"Children, sometimes when you've been studying a mentor author for a very specific thing, like in this case, how Cynthia Rylant creates patterns of three, you want to give that work a try while it's fresh in your mind. Before we leave the rug, why don't you look over your stories, and see if you can find at least one place where you might add a pattern. When you've got it, show your partner, and then quick as a bunny, off to your desk to get one done before you forget. Then you'll have your own example of a pattern that stretches out a part of your story. Of course, later in workshop, you can work on all the parts of your story that you want to get written today as well."

I waited until writers had found a spot, and sent them off one by one to get to it.

While most of your links have offered choice, sometimes it's helpful to set students to a strategy task while the example is fresh in their minds. This is probably one of those times.

Coaching Writers to Help Build Independence

TODAY, YOU PROBABLY WON'T CONFER AROUND THE MINILESSON, as some of your writers will have more urgent writing goals than writing patterns that will merit your attention. Instead, you might consider supporting your students who continue to be reluctant writers, ones who struggle to come up with ideas for stories. One strategy that can help some children is to have them imagine an episode with characters they know from a television show or series. This strategy sometimes gets reluctant writers started. It's almost as if they can jump on the writing train because someone else started the engine.

In this case, Zahir said he wanted to write a fiction story that featured Henry and Mudge. He didn't want to make up his own characters this time. He wanted to add a lost episode to this famous collection. So we looked at a Henry and Mudge book together for inspiration. I asked, "What will happen to Henry and Mudge in your book?" He said, "They will go to the beach." So I pointed out the chapter titles in our mentor text and said, "Have you thought about how yours would go?" I was hoping my question would encourage planning.

Zahir said, "They will play at the beach." I quickly jotted "Chapter One . . . Chapter Two . . . Chapter Three" as a starting point. After a little more thinking, Zahir decided on the following.

> Chapter One Henry and Mudge go to the beach
> Chapter Two Surfboard at the beach
> Chapter Three Playing in the sand

Zahir's chapter titles served as a plan. Since he was ready to begin, I decided to leave him to work on it.

MID-WORKSHOP TEACHING
Using Patterns to Stretch Out Endings

"Writers, eyes on me. I want to acknowledge Alejandra. Alejandra used a pattern for the ending of her story! At first she ended her story simply with, 'There was a storm.' Then she tried to add a pattern of three, and listen to this." I read aloud Alejandra's writing (see Figure 14–1).

When Milkey and her family got home the storm began with thunder, rain, and worse of all . . . LIGHTNING!!! But it was good they got home before the storm.

FIG. 14–1   Alejandra's pattern at the ending of her piece creates story tension!

"Maybe you'll want to try this too.

"I also want to acknowledge Avery. Avery also used a pattern to stretch out his ending so it's more exciting. In Avery's story, his character Joshua gets lost at the zoo and looks for his mom. At first the end of his story went like this." I picked up Avery's story and read (see Figure 14–2).

> Then Joshua looked around for his mom but his mom wasn't to be found. "Oh No!" cried Joshua, "where is my mom?" Joshua looked in the door and found his mom.

I looked up at the children. "But then after some clever revision work of adding more details *and* thinking about a pattern, Avery used a pattern to stretch out this part of his story. So now it reads:

> Joshua looked into the door. "No signs of mom," whispered Joshua. Then Joshua went inside the door to find his mom. Then Joshua was inside and he saw his mom! He ran to her and gave her a big hug.

"Isn't that clever, how Avery used a pattern of three to stretch out that part of his story? It really makes his ending exciting.

"Right now, look at your own ending and see if using a pattern of three to stretch out the action or to stretch out a feeling will help make your story more exciting. Go ahead, play with a pattern for your ending!

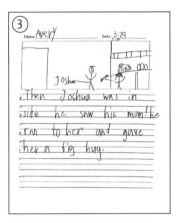

FIG. 14–2 Avery revised his ending by including a pattern to stretch it out.

A bit later, I asked Zahir if I could see his story about Henry and Mudge at the beach. Zahir had, indeed, planned out his chapters, and he had written them as well. When I looked at the chapters, though, he had only two or three sentences in each chapter. Now that Zahir had a story, the time seemed ripe to remind him of the work we had done with patterns. I started by asking, "Which part in the story do you want to add more?" I knew that if I offered choice about *where* to add words, he would be less likely to resist going back and adding more words later. Zahir chose Chapter Three.

Before the conference Zahir had written:

Chapter Three–Playing in the sand

Then Henry played in the sand. He made a sandcastle. Henry was looking for shells.

I invited Zahir to think back over a couple of the ways he had learned to stretch out parts of his stories, especially patterns. Knowing that reluctant writers often benefit from acting out parts of their story, I encouraged Zahir to incorporate acting out as he played with patterns. Zahir and I looked closely again at the pages in *Henry and*

Mudge and the Happy Cat. Then I moved my body in a way that resembled looking for shells and making a sandcastle as written in Zahir's book. He was shy to act at first, so I acted with him. As I pretended I was looking for shells I said, "Okay, what now? What else can you say about Henry playing in the sand? Be like Cynthia Rylant! Give Henry some patterns!"

Zahir said, "He found different shells."

I said, "Be *more* like Cynthia Rylant. Say three things!"

He added, "He found snail shells, crab shells, and starfish."

"*Wow*, you are on a roll! Keep going. What did he say or do next?"

Zahir paused to think and then added, "Henry said, 'Playing in the sand is fun!'"

"Write this down, Zahir, you have a wonderful pattern!" I finished the conference by having Zahir say back what work he had done to get to this new writing that he could do next time on his own. "Well," he said, "I can ask myself, 'What else can I add? Should I add some patterns? Should I act it out? What would Cynthia Rylant do?'" (See Figure 14–3.)

① To the Henry and beach. Mudge go at the beach.
Name: Zahir   Date: 4/18

It was a hot day. Henry want to go at the beach. So Henry tell his mom. Henry mom said yes. Henry was happy.

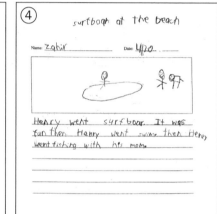
② Name: Zahir   Date: 4/19

Henry and Mudge and Henry mom went to the beach. Henry want to take his surfboar.

③ Name: Zahir   Date: 4/19

When they got at the beach they saw lot of people some people was in the water. Some people were playing in the sand.

④ surfboar at the beach
Name: Zahir   Date: 4/20

Henry went surfboar. It was fun then Henry went swim then Henry went fishing with his mom.

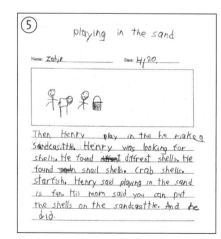
⑤ playing in the sand
Name: Zahir   Date: 4/20

Then Henry play in the he make a sandcasttle. Henry was looking for shells. He found diffrent shells. He found snail shells. Crab shells. starfish. Henry said playing in the sand is fun. His mom said you can put the shells on the sandcasttle. And he did.

FIG. 14–3 Zahir imagines a story in a familiar series as one of his own stories. Here, he writes a "missing episode" from the Henry and Mudge series.

Making Reading and Writing Connections in Just-Right Books

Have students find patterns in their independent reading books, transferring the strategies they are learning in writing workshop to their reading.

"Writers, we are going to do something different in today's share session. Today, instead of bringing just your writing I would like you to bring your reading baggies and a couple of Post-its to the meeting area." They scurried around to gather their books, excited about the change.

"So, today we looked together at the patterns Cynthia Rylant wrote in *Henry and Mudge and the Happy Cat*. But writers, *lots* of authors play with patterns. You might find even more ideas, from the authors you are reading. Let's see what happens when you look for patterns in your book baggies. Take out a book, and when you notice a pattern place a Post-it on the page so you will be ready to share it with your partner."

While children looked for patterns, I listened in and coached them. After a few minutes, I invited kids to share.

Nora held up *Poppleton*. "Listen to this," she said, "It's about Poppleton's new house in the country." She read, "It had a little sunroom where Poppleton took naps. It had lots and lots of shelves where Poppleton kept things. It had a little garden where Poppleton planted corn. And it had Cherry Sue." Nora waved the book, insisting on our attention. "Do you hear the three? It's got three! A sunroom, shelves, and a garden."

"Hold on, Nora, can you read that for us again? Children, listen like detectives, what do you notice about the pattern?" Nora read again. "Turn and talk, writers, what did you notice?" The children began to turn and talk, though Nora, too excited to wait, broke in quickly with, "It breaks the pattern! I read a book like that last night to my little brother." She recited, "I've read that book a thousand times. It goes . . . the truck is red, the bike is red, the car is red . . . the house is yellow."

The children nodded, still familiar with this kind of pattern book.

"Hmm . . . you could do that too, writers! You might decide to break from your pattern as you write the last, or third, detail in your pattern. What I really love, though, is how you are seeing so much more in your books, because you are reading like writers."

Writers Use Their Superpowers to Work with Greater Independence

IN THIS SESSION, you'll remind students that writers use all their superpowers—everything they know and have learned about a type of writing—to get better.

GETTING READY

✔ A superhero to reference in the connection, for example Spiderman, and pictures of the superhero to share with the class (see Connection)

✔ Access to all the tools kids have been using, such as charts, folders, books, and so on to reference during the lesson (see Guided Inquiry)

✔ "The Super Writing Powers of Super Series Writers" list, prewritten with writing powers you think your students will find in the classroom (see Guided Inquiry)

COMMON CORE STATE STANDARDS: W.1.3, W.1.5, W.1.8, W.2.3, RL.1.1, RL.1.3, SL.1.1, L.1.1, L.1.2

THIS SESSION MARKS ONE OF THOSE DELIBERATE PAUSES in a unit of study, where you give children a chance to apply the strategies they have been learning. Our consistent attention to these moments in these units of study stems from the Common Core State Standards' emphasis on independent application and from Norman Webb's Depth of Knowledge work. To allow for transference, this final session in the bend is a recall/inquiry lesson, where students will take the lead in recalling and synthesizing all they have learned so far in the unit.

When we choose transference moments, we often choose moments when we're sure students have enough writing to do, and enough strategies to play with, that they can forge ahead without new instruction—when, in fact, it may be a good time to hold off for a moment on any new strategies while you watch your students apply what they've been taught so far. Your students should have plenty to do with all the stories they are writing for their series, and they have plenty of new skills to apply (and old ones learned during the *Small Moments* unit). So in this lesson, you'll develop children's sense of agency—of them taking charge, of wanting to practice, of demonstrating expertise.

This is also a good time for you to assess whether and how the teaching charts and learning tools you've been making for the classroom continue to be helpful for your students. Watch them study your bulletin boards and charts, their checklists, and their folders. You'll learn a lot about how they are processing the materials in the room as extra instructional tools. If any charts seem to be ignored, it might be time to take them down. If others light the children with energy, put those back out, front and center.

There is power in classroom metaphors, which is why this session doesn't just say "use the strategies you know," but refers to "superpowers." If you really want to be campy, you could have little red capes for students to wear or wands of power, to help them step into their roles of superheroes. You could have pictures of superheroes, or clips from *Schoolhouse Rock!* Children will probably do a better job if you make this dramatic. Role-playing their way into being powerful writers works just as well as role-playing themselves into a character.

Writers Use Their Superpowers to Work with Greater Independence

CONNECTION

Make an allusion to a superhero (it could be Spiderman or another popular superhero your children know well) as someone students can be like if they choose to access their powers as well.

"Writers, gather around, I have a few pictures here to show you." I slowly pulled from behind my back an image of Peter Parker in his school clothes. Then I pulled out another, of him as Spiderman in his spider suit. I could hear the children whisper "Spiderman" to each other.

"Children, I think many of you know Spiderman. Spiderman has superpowers. He can swing from tall buildings, he can spin webs, and he can even rescue anyone in danger!"

The children nodded. One or two put a thumb up for the pattern of three, which made me laugh. "Well, children, the thing about Spiderman is that when he puts on his spider suit, he uses all his secret superpowers. He has these powers all the time, even when he's ordinary Peter Parker, but it's like, when he puts on the suit, he becomes . . . *super*." I made my voice strong and loud for the word *super*, and the children giggled. "When Spiderman swings around, doing super things, he is using all his powers."

I put down the pictures. "Writers do this too. They don't have to sit around waiting for someone to tell them what to do. They use all their powers, just like Spiderman."

I slumped over, looking tired and helpless. "Join me for a moment, writers. Before we take on the role of superwriters, let's be helpless writers—real Peter Parkers. We're going to whine and act helpless, as if we have no idea what to do next." I bent my head over and began to say in a low, whiny voice, "Where's the paper? I don't have a pencil. I can't think of any ideas. I don't know what to do." The kids chimed in, giggling and whining. "My partner is absent. I can't remember how to show, not tell. I don't know what to add next. *I have to go to the bathroom*," they chorused the final refrain with me.

◆ COACHING

We use Peter Parker because, at this writing, Spiderman is big in children's books, television shows, and movies. If your children have another favorite hero (ask them), use that persona to symbolize a superhero—but it might be important to choose someone who is sometimes ordinary and sometimes extraordinary, so you can contrast those ways of being.

Making comparisons to popular culture helps engage students, and sometimes it also helps them understand metaphor. Saying "I want you to be like Spiderman" sounds a lot more exciting than "I want you to use the writing strategies I taught you." You can also increase engagement by calling on familiar rituals. Earlier in the unit, for instance, you did some role-playing of the helpless writer—now that can be the Peter Parker writer.

GUIDED INQUIRY

Name a question that will guide the inquiry.

"Writers, today we are going to do an inquiry—we're going to investigate an important question. The question we are going to ask is, 'What super writing powers do I have, as a super series writer?'"

Set students up to look around the room at charts, bulletin boards, folders, and books to guide them in finding their superpowers.

"Writers, are you asking yourself that question? 'What super powers do I have as a super series writer?'" I waited a moment. "I see you nodding, children, but I don't see you answering! What are those superpowers, writers? Where are they hiding? Can you remember them all?

"The thing about superpowers, children, is that they don't do you any good if you don't remember them! So right now, let's investigate the answer to your question. Imagine this whole room is a treasure chest. Look around, at the charts, and bulletin boards, and books, look in your folders, and find evidence of your super powers. Like I'm seeing . . . " I turned to the anchor chart from Bend I. "One of my super powers is . . . the power to create pretend characters!" I stood tall, and proclaimed, "I can create pretend characters. Ha!

"Go forth, young investigators! Look for reminders in your folders, on the walls—try to find something you know how to do as a writer that makes you super-duper. Go, young spiderchildren! You have two minutes to find a power."

I made my voice very dramatic for that last bit. As some children waited uncertainly, I voiced over to help them. "I see Jack returning to his secret storage place. *What* will he find there? Etta is moving toward some old teaching charts from our *Small Moments* unit. Who knows what secrets she'll uncover? Will she find how to . . . start a story? Unfreeze characters?"

One of the great joys of teaching young children is the joy of dramatic role-play. Children love when you make work into play. Bring in a tablecloth cape, proclaim your super powers, swing into action as a super teacher. Whether you imagine yourself as Xena, Wonder Woman, or the Incredible Hulk, the image you carry in your mind's eye will inspire your followers.

Listen in to your investigators and jot a list (or get ready to unroll one you've made earlier that will look as if you made it now).

As the children began calling out from corners of the room, I assembled a list quickly.

The Super Writing Powers of Super Series Writers

✓ We set goals.
✓ We create pretend characters.
✓ We invent adventures for our characters.
✓ We get characters into trouble . . . and out of trouble.
✓ We unfreeze people.
✓ We add tiny, realistic details.
✓ We make chapters for our stories.
✓ We use patterns to stretch parts.
✓ We study our mentor authors.
✓ We spell the best we can.

LINK

Help students organize themselves to get started with agency and superpowers.

After calling students back to the meeting area, I said, "Writers! This is quite a list of super powers. I'm expecting great things of you today as writers.

"I'm going to admire you as you work hard at writing like the superstars you really are. Today, and every day from now on, remember that you have superpowers inside you. Before you go off to write, tell your partner which superpowers you are really going to try to use today. You might choose something from this list or you may have your own, personal power." I gave partners just a moment to talk, and then set them off to write.

Of course, while you are researching your students, you could also have much of this list already written and ready to secretly unfold, so that you feel ready. Teachers need their secret powers, too!

Making Our First-Draft Writing Stronger

DURING INDEPENDENT WRITING TIME TODAY, you will want to keep going with the idea that your students are using powers as they write more and keep themselves going with more independence. But you might also think of today's conferring as a time to focus on writers you've had your eye on, who you know would benefit from targeted small-group instruction or one-on-one conferring. You might consider taking a look at your students' on-demand work from the beginning of this unit (or their on-demand pieces from the *Small Moments* unit) to collect the data you need to see how your students are improving and where they might need help. If your students haven't been showing signs of improvement, you'll take that as feedback that your teaching has not been sticking with them, and you'll want to make it a priority to find out immediately how you can help these writers improve leaps and bounds in the remaining week of the unit. I had my eye on a couple of writers even before I knew what they were doing, exactly. The reason I was thinking of these writers was I had been watching their habits over the last couple of weeks, and I was waiting for an opportunity to really have enough data in hand to coach them personally. Today, I called over Maeve and Syanna. Both of these writers sometimes left a lot of work for revision, especially punctuation and capitals. Maeve, for instance, had just written the first page of a new story. (See Figure 15–1.) It started:

> One fall day a girl named Mora was watching TV. She said Let's watch pussy cats on TV. She was with her sister and her big sister. She was feeling well, until her mom said we are going to get a Bike for your sister. What?

"Maeve," I said, "let's sit for a moment with your partner. I've been thinking about you as a writer—in fact, I went back and looked at your on-demand small moment that you did at the end of our *Small Moments* unit, and the on-demand story you wrote at the beginning of this unit. And you know what I noticed? I noticed that sometimes you are not revising your writing as you go, and you are missing things that you know how to do as a writer. Let me give you an example." I took out her writing pieces, and had

her put her most recent story on her desk as well. "Let's just look at the dialogue in your stories. Each time, you are putting speech bubbles in your pictures—that's great. I love how your characters talk. And then, you put some of what your characters say into the story too." I pointed to some of her sentences. "And then Maeve, when you revise, you add in quotations for your dialogue." I pointed to where Maeve had added in some dialogue quotation marks, in a different color pen.

"Maeve, I think you're becoming the kind of writer who can add dialogue right into your story, and punctuate it as well, as you're writing. I don't think you have to wait to do this smart work. Does that sound right to you?" Maeve nodded. "I'm guessing you already know something about how to write dialogue, and how to punctuate dialogue too?" Slowly, Maeve nodded, looking at some of her revisions.

MID-WORKSHOP TEACHING   Silent Cheer Shout-Outs!

"Writers, oh, I mean, *superwriters*! I would like to check in to see how you are all doing. So I will call out a super writing power from our list, and as I do, if you are using that power raise your arms in the air and give a silent cheer!

"Okay, ready? We use patterns." Arms went flying up to cheer. "We add tiny, realistic details!" The cheers continued. "We spell the best we can!"

I continued with a few more and then said, "Wait a second, writers. How do I know you're not really being Peter Parkers? Right now, find a part of your writing where there is evidence of your superpowers, and show your partner that part!"

"I'm going to watch you get started, Maeve, on the next part of your story. If you find that you want to make your characters talk, this time I'll be curious how you go from speech bubbles to dialogue with quotation marks."

I left Maeve to keep working, and in a few moments, revisited her. On the next page of her story, she had written:

> "We need to get a bike for your sister." "NO, I want to watch TV.
> Well you can't right now.

This was a good start. Maeve was now moving the dialogue from her speech bubbles down into her story on her first draft, and she was beginning to punctuate her dialogue more accurately as well. "Maeve," I said. "It's great that you are taking something that you used to do in revision, and now you are doing it when you write for the first time! That's a super powerful move as a writer. Maybe you could teach Syanna some of what you've learned, about figuring out what you've been doing in revision, and starting to write like that when you write for the first time? I have Syanna's on-demand pieces here as well, and you could study them."

I left the girls poring over their prior writing, comparing what they had done to the writing they were doing now. In this way, the girls were learning to make their first draft writing stronger. They were also learning that who they were as writers was changing, and they could be in charge of becoming even stronger writers.

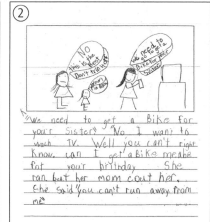

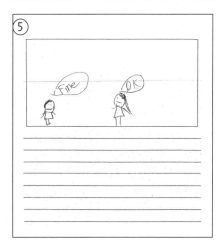

FIG. 15–1   Here, Maeve learns to move from "waiting for revision" before doing her best writing, such as adding and punctuating dialogue, to doing her best when she writes for the first time.

Questions to Push Our Thinking

Invite students to share their writing and explore questions to push their thinking.

"Writers, as you come to the meeting area bring one of your stories that you would especially like to talk about and share with others." As the kids gathered, I wrote a few questions on a chart for us to refer to.

> Did anyone try anything new and difficult today?
> Did anyone tackle any new and hard challenges?
> Did anyone invent new powers?

I read aloud the questions and said, "Let's explore these questions. Take a moment, and if you have something to share, give a thumbs up." Lots of thumbs went up, so I said, "Turn and talk to your partner, asking each other these questions."

Philip said, "I made sure my character's name Max started with a capital letter every time."

Heather said, "I added more to my pictures, like Cynthia Rylant."

Then I pulled the class back together. "Writers, you are describing some of the important work you did. Now I have an extra challenge. You did important work, but was it hard? Can you really say it was new, or hard, or difficult? Talk to your partner again. In fact, you might even read this list," I pointed to our Super Writing Powers list, "and say 'easy' or 'hard' for each item."

They did so. After a moment, I gathered their attention. "Writers, eyes on me. You know in reading, how you are always working on getting a lot of reading done, and reading harder and harder books, so you can become a super reader? Well it's the same with writing, you want to get a lot of writing done, and you want to work on harder and harder things.

"Right now, before we end, will you think, 'What could I do as a writer that would be hard for me? That would really challenge me?' And can you say what that thing is, to your partner? Turn and talk."

I listened in as the children talked about trying sparkle words, writing a really long story, and creating a new pretend character. "Let's take a few minutes, right now, so you can try the work that you've chosen. Go to it, superwriters."

Punctuation Parties

IN THIS SESSION, you'll teach students that writers work hard on revising their stories, which includes using fabulous punctuation.

GETTING READY

✔ Fiction book to show how punctuation impacts a storyteller's voice. We use *Harry by the Sea*. (see Connection)

✔ Punctuation Post-its (a collection of Post-its, each with an exclamation mark or question mark or period drawn in very bright green) (see Teaching and Active Engagement)

✔ Two parts of your own story written on chart paper, with blanks for ending punctuation. You'll want to use the same series character you used in Bend III. (see Teaching and Active Engagement)

✔ Punctuation pens (special green markers reserved for adding/fixing punctuation) (see Link)

COMMON CORE STATE STANDARDS: W.1.3, W.1.5, W.2.3, RL.1.1, RFS.1.1, RFS.1.4, SL.1.1, SL.1.6, L.1.1.j,g; L.1.2.b

YOUR FIRST-GRADERS are approaching their publishing date and you'll want to play up the upcoming publication of their second series as a big event. Mark this event with stars on your calendar. Take some time for children to write invitations to their celebration—the publication of the long awaited new series by . . . You might make a poster like those found in bookstores, announcing the preorder or upcoming publication of a particular series. You might make a podcast of interviews with your authors. Playing up the drama of approaching publication reminds young writers that they are writing for real audiences. It gives them reasons to polish their writing. This is a good time to talk about who the audience actually will be—will it be parents? Will they be reading and showing their writing to kindergartners, or to older students? Children write with more urgency and agency when they are not writing for one teacher, but for specific, authentic audiences they care about. Sometimes picking a real person (a buddy from another grade, a sibling, a classmate, a family member) and dedicating the book to that person, helps a writer say, "Wow, I want so and so to be able to read my words. I want to do my best work!"

As you inspire your writers to write for readers, inspire them with the creative work of publication as well—color illustrations, the order of their series, blurbs for the back, and so on. Once again, you'll want to have on hand the materials for revisions, and the materials for publishing boxed sets. Boxes, paint, pictures of the author, strips, flaps, extra pages, and colored pens will all inspire your writers. They'll use these materials over the next few sessions for their punctuation work, illustrations, and spelling, as well as the acknowledgments, dedications, and author profiles that delight young writers.

Today's session particularly invites your writers to play with and revise their ending punctuation. A number of years ago, *Schoolhouse Rock!* used to have spots on Saturday morning television. "Lolly, Lolly, Lolly Get Your Adverb Here!" and "Conjunction Junction, What's Your Function?" made learning grammar a delight. Rhymes and songs helped a generation remember that a noun is a person, place, or thing. The same attention to *how* children learn that went into *Sesame Street*, and later into shows like *Blues Clues*, went into the *Schoolhouse Rock!* videos. In his study of *Sesame Street*, in *The Tipping Point*, Malcolm Gladwell gave the name "stickiness" to this kind of instruction, because it literally stuck in children's minds.

"They'll play with ending punctuation today, exploring the intent of it, which is to guide the reader's voice and emotions."

That's what we're aiming for here—a sense of stickiness, the kind of stickiness that comes with play, repetition, and engagement. This is your mission: To get children to work with ending punctuation, but rather than "fixing" mistakes, you'll entice children to play. They'll play with ending punctuation today, exploring the intent of it, which is to guide the reader's voice and emotions.

You'll also shamelessly exploit the delight children take in using special markers. There is something about a beautiful Sharpie or fine-point architect's pen that makes anyone want to use it and use it well. Here, you'll have some special "punctuation pens" that are reserved for the sole purpose of working on end punctuation. Kept back for this purpose, in a special container, these pens enhance the urge to punctuate with purpose.

Punctuation Parties

CONNECTION

Stir your students up to get excited to publish their series.

"Come close, writers. We are entering a special time now. It's almost time to get ready to publish your second series. I can't wait to see the final boxed sets. I can already picture them." I made my voice dramatic. "Another famous series by Miles. The second series by well-known author Annabel."

Make the link from getting ready to publish to thinking about and fixing up ending punctuation. Then refer to a recent time when you read aloud and your voice didn't match the ending punctuation.

"We all know that to get your series books ready to publish, you need to revise and edit your stories so they are as *fabulous* as possible. After all, this is your second series, and you are superwriters!

"Well, writers, remember how we had a revision party for our first series? Today we are going to have a special revision party—a punctuation party!

"You might be asking yourself: Why punctuation? Does punctuation deserve a party?" I paused, looking around with a doubting look on my face. Then I affirmed, "Yes it does! Punctuation matters. In fact, let me tell you a punctuation story.

"Yesterday, I was reading aloud *Harry by the Sea*, the one where he goes to the seaside and gets covered in seaweed.

"Well, I was reading to my nephew, Graham, and I was tired. So as I read the story I was sounding kind of sleepy." I let my voice get slow and low and sleepy as I said this. "I got to the part where Harry gets covered in seaweed and people think he's a monster. 'It's a sea monster,'" I murmured in a slow, sleepy voice, with no drama or inflection.

"Well, my nephew poked me and said, 'You're reading it wrong. It's supposed to sound exciting.' It's supposed to sound like 'It's a *Sea Monster!*' Then he pointed to the exclamation mark. 'See?' he said. 'That means it's supposed to be exciting.'"

Children love to be referred to in a minilesson, and it's much more time-efficient than calling on them. Be strategic, and you'll have some reluctant writers glowing at your references.

When you hearken back to prior teaching and rituals you help foster a sense of continuity. Here, you recall the revision party, setting up a new kind of revision party—a punctuation party. The language of play continues to position revision as a joyful challenge, a lifelong attitude to foster.

Play up how important punctuation is for the reader. Stir up your writers to want their punctuation to be fabulous.

"Writers, my nephew reminded me how important punctuation is. That little exclamation mark makes sure the reader knows this is an exciting part, that people are *shouting!*"

❖ **Name the teaching point.**

"Writers, today I want to teach you that writers use punctuation to give orders to their readers. One way writers make sure their punctuation is giving the right orders is to reread part of their story out loud, and when they want a part to sound *exciting*, they add an exclamation mark. When they want a part to sound like the character is questioning or wondering, they add a question mark."

TEACHING

Set students up to watch you demonstrate how to read aloud part of your writing and add in punctuation that matches your storytelling voice. Introduce your story so students are ready for the part you'll focus on.

"Writers often fix up their punctuation when they revise. Watch me do this work by reading aloud a part of my story. In this story, Sam took his neighbor's poodle Snowball to the store and tied her up. When he came out of the store, there were two poodles. They looked just alike!" The children giggled.

"Here's the part of my story where Sam wanted to tie Snowball up."

I gestured to the chart.

> Snowball's fur was so puffy that Sam couldn't find her collar.
> "Where oh where is your collar ___" Sam asked Snowball.
> Snowball licked Sam's face.
> "No licking ___" Sam said. Snowball licked him again.
> "No licking ___" Sam shouted.
> "What should I do ___" Sam asked himself.
> If he didn't tie Snowball up, she would run away ____

I gestured to the collection of Post-its that were lined up along the side of the chart. "Watch as I read the story the way I want it to sound and how I choose a punctuation Post-it to help my reader."

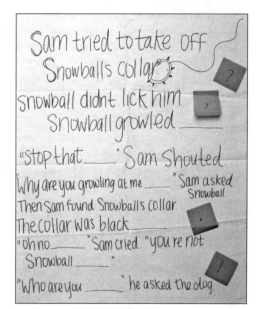

Demonstrate making punctuation choices, slowing down the work so that students can hear and see how you make these choices.

I started to read, and as I did so, I exaggerated my voice so that Sam sounded *very* unsure and questioning for the questions and *very* excited for the exclamations. As I did so, I thought aloud about my punctuation choices, saying things like "Hmm, I want Sam to sound really excited here, so . . . exclamation mark it is! Here, Sam is really questioning what to do." I placed the matching punctuation Post-its on the chart as I worked.

Next I gestured to the punctuation Post-its now marking my story, and I read it aloud again, pointing to the punctuation as I read. The children watched and listened to my voice. I could see them pointing to the punctuation Post-its as I read.

ACTIVE ENGAGEMENT

Invite students to help you add punctuation to another part of your story. Emphasize that this is important work.

"I'd love to have you come to my punctuation party! You can help me fix up another part of my story by adding in punctuation. I've got another part of my story on chart paper, and you can see the punctuation Post-its lined up along the side. This time, I'm going to read the story aloud, the way I want it to sound. How about if you and your partner listen and then help me decide which punctuation Post-its should go where. It's the part of my story where Sam realized he had the wrong dog." I flipped my chart paper to the next page, showing:

> Sam tried to take off Snowball's collar.
> Snowball didn't lick him. Snowball growled ___
> "Stop that ___" Sam shouted.
> "Why are you growling at me ___" Sam asked Snowball.
> Then Sam found Snowball's collar.
> The collar was black ___
> "Oh no ___" Sam cried. "You're not Snowball ___"
> "Who are you ___" he asked the dog.

I read the story aloud, exaggerating, again, the excitement when an exclamation point was called for and the questioning tone when a question mark was called for. The children began to whisper to each other and point to the punctuation Post-it choices.

As partners turn and talk, invite a few to move the punctuation Post-its on the chart.

"Go ahead, writers, talk to your partner. Which punctuation Post-its would you put where?"

The children did so. I signaled a few kids to dash up to the easel and move specific punctuation marks into the story.

Miles put a "?" after "Why are you growling at me?"

Alejandra and her partner decided on an "!" for both "Oh no!" and "You're not Snowball!"

Then I called everyone's attention.

Read the story again, pointing to the punctuation Post-its as you read.

"Look at the story now, writers. What a great start to our punctuation party. Now the punctuation will really help my reader's voice sound right. No sleepy readers' voices here, because our punctuation gives clear orders to the reader! Let's read the story again, together." We read it in a chorus, with great drama. I pointed to the punctuation as we read.

LINK

Send the children off, emphasizing that adding punctuation is an essential part of getting ready to publish. Offer up your punctuation pens as enticement.

"Writers, this week, as you get your series ready for publishing, I know you're going to want to revise your punctuation. Here's one special tip. There is something about using a fabulous color that gets writers excited about adding ending punctuation to their writing. You see how my Post-its were all green? Well, I have some special punctuation pens over here. They're only for writers who are revising ending punctuation. When you want to do this work, come get a special punctuation pen, and feel the excitement! Off you go, and if you're revising punctuation today, come by for a punctuation pen! If you have other writing work to do, you can get a pen later."

Using Mentor Sentences to Teach Punctuation

TODAY DURING CONFERRING you will most likely want to keep the focus on helping kids prepare for the upcoming celebration. So you can be on the lookout for kids who need your support with revising and editing in general, but most of all help with punctuation. Here are a few things to look out for as you research today.

You will probably see the typical period at the end of every line or one every two or three words or a classic favorite, one *big* giant one at the very end of the page. You may even see kids making the end mark so light you can't even see it. Let's not forget those with no sign of any punctuation.

In addition, you may only see periods and not varied punctuation like the exclamation marks or question marks mentioned in today's lesson. And, conversely, you may also see exclamation points or question marks all over some students' writing, with no apparent purpose.

You may also have kids using punctuation without starting the next sentence with a capital letter. Finally, be ready to teach kids already using end marks fairly well things like quotation marks and commas.

After you have researched, you can group kids with similar needs and pull them for a small-group session. Have a few mentor sentences ready, and ask kids to cross-check their sentences with the mentor sentences. You can design your mentor sentences to match what the kids need. Feel free to write your

own or pull them from a mentor text the kids know well, like *Henry and Mudge and the Happy Cat*.

You may also want to do a small group version of the work done in the minilesson. In this case, you can use small Post-its for the end punctuation marks, and kids can place them directly on their own writing. These gimmicks often help!

And remember, reading aloud helps with end punctuation, so encourage kids to read aloud as they work on their punctuation. Syanna, for instance, read aloud her own writing to her partner, Maeve. As they got to the part of her story about a scary visit to the doctor where the Mom said, "You tricked me," Syanna read in an excited, almost yelling voice. As I listened in, I prompted Maeve to help Syanna with the ending punctuation. "You need to put some exclamation marks there!" Maeve noted. Syanna set to work, adding one exclamation mark where the voice would rise, and several where the voice would really rise.

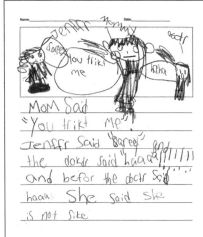

FIG. 16–1   Syanna adds punctuation after reading her story aloud to her partner.

MID-WORKSHOP TEACHING
Using Ellipses to Create Suspense

"Writers, I need to interrupt the party. I thought you might all like to see what Annabel did. Annabel was writing about a time when her character was at the zoo, and she used a special form of punctuation, the 'dot, dot, dot.'" I jotted " . . . " on a whiteboard for students to see.

"Listen to this." I read aloud, "'Suddenly her stuffed Bear was gone. She looked everywhere. She looked in the bathroom. She looked in the cafeteria. And then she saw it. Bear was in . . . (dot, dot, dot) the monkey's cage!'

"Isn't that clever, using dot, dot, dot for an exciting part? It slows down the readers' voice. You might want to play with that punctuation too, writers."

Classmates Are Mentors Too

Highlight one or two writers who have done solid work on ending punctuation today, to serve as mentors as students continue to revise and edit their fiction books for publication.

"Writers, please bring your writing to the meeting area and let's share any clever punctuation in your stories. To get us started, let's take a close look at Sophia's fiction book." I read the piece aloud, pausing at the punctuation and pointing out the varied punctuation in her story (see Figure 16–2).

Page 1: What's the matter? My favorite blanket is ruined, said Melissa.

Page 2: Where is it? Over here Melissa said. It has a hole. Oh no! (in speech bubble)

Page 3: Her mom got the needle and thread and started sewing.

Page 4: It is ok said Melissa's mom. I'll just sew!

Page 5: Here you go Melissa! YAY! (in speech bubble)

FIG. 16–2   Sophia's fiction book. Sophia revised her punctuation to add question marks and exclamation marks to guide her reader.

"Now let's take a look at Nandika's first page of her fiction book" (see Figure 16–3). I read Nandika's story aloud, with drama, and showed students the first page. "Turn and tell your partner any punctuation you notice Nandika using just on page 1!" I listened in as students pointed and talked.

> One day Rosie was wiggling her tooth. All of a sudden her tooth started bleeding! "My tooth is bleeding!" she screamed. Her mother came running. "Are you Okay?" her mother asked. "No," cried Rosie. "My tooth is bleeding."

"Writers, a few of you noticed that Nandika had some very fancy punctuation for dialogue. You learned how to do that way back in our *Small Moments* unit. See how she has quotation marks, and ending punctuation? That way her reader will know to read in the character's voice.

"Writers, to celebrate your punctuation, and make sure it's doing the work you want, let's switch books with your partner. Listen to your partner read your book. Especially listen for the power of your punctuation!"

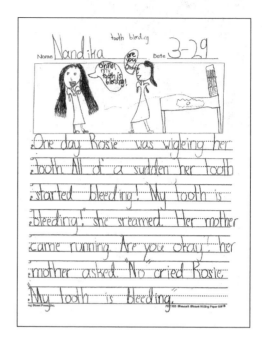

FIG. 16–3   Page 1 of Nandika's fiction book shows Nandika using ending punctuation to add to the drama of her story. She also punctuates her dialogue accurately.

Writers Use Illustrations to Tell Important Details

THIS SESSION IS ANOTHER ONE OF THOSE where you increase engagement by tackling something that you're pretty sure most of your students will love, and tuck in some serious teaching as you do.

Your students have learned to sketch early on in the writing process, as a means of planning and rehearsing. Along the way, they've probably also added details to their writing by first adding details to their sketches. Some children have probably added cover illustrations and other color pictures to their stories, making this connection because they mostly read stories with pictures and they think of pictures as integral to stories.

In this session, you'll investigate the role that illustrations play in the stories kids read and write. Just think of *Knuffle Bunny*—how much of the story happens through the pictures! Or think back to *Good Night Moon* and how the clock in the room moves forward, and the mouse and kittens play, and the balloon rises—all of which happens in the pictures, giving the reader even more to notice and delight in.

If your classroom is low on books you can structure this lesson so that you investigate the roles that illustrations play in your mentor text. Or, you can conduct a more extended inquiry, handing out a variety of favorite stories, including ones from children's independent reading, picture books from read-aloud, and perhaps early childhood favorites such as *Goodnight Moon*. If you do the latter, you might want to read *Knuffle Bunny* aloud prior to this session, since the pictures play such a delightful and significant role in that story.

Either way, this session supports students in working toward the Common Core reading standards as well as the writing standards. It's not until third grade that the Common Core State Standards expect readers to analyze and compare what is told in pictures versus text in fiction. But there is no reason not to start that work now, when the opportunity is at hand. After this session, your children are sure to be more alert to the details of the illustrations in the stories they read, and eager to revise their own stories, by adding important details to their pictures.

IN THIS SESSION, you'll teach children that writers use illustrations in important ways, and you'll investigate the roles illustrations play by studying them in mentor texts.

GETTING READY

✔ A favorite text that uses pictures to convey information to the reader, to reference in the connection. We use *Knuffle Bunny* by Mo Willems.

✔ A mentor text you have been using that has details in the pictures that are not in the words. We use *Henry and Mudge and the Happy Cat.*

✔ Pages from the mentor text displayed (or enough copies of the book to share) for students to study in partnerships. These pages should have detailed illustrations that show what is happening in the story. (see Active Engagement)

✔ "Our Favorite Series Authors . . . " chart from Session 9, to add to during the active engagement

✔ Students' favorite read-aloud books, their independent reading books, and other mentor texts for them to mine for illustration ideas (see Share)

COMMON CORE STATE STANDARDS: W.1.3, W.1.5, W.2.3, RL.1.1, RL.1.4, RL.1.7, SL.1.1, SL.1.5, L.1.1, L.1.2

Writers Use Illustrations to Tell Important Details

CONNECTION

Make a reference to a favorite text that uses pictures, instead of words, to convey information to the reader.

"Writers, come close. I want to show you something. You remember how I sometimes read aloud to my nephew, Graham? Well, yesterday we were reading aloud *Knuffle Bunny*." I held it up, and the children all laughed at the familiar picture of Trixie, her harried father, and the soon-to-be-lost stuffed toy.

"Well, children, I got to this page." I held up the famous page where Knuffle Bunny, unbeknownst to Daddy, is left behind at the Laundromat. "I read it aloud." I did so. "And Graham pointed to the picture and said, 'That's where Knuffle Bunny gets left behind.'"

Call children's attention to the details the reader finds out only through the pictures, and alert children that they can do the same work in their stories, as part of their revision.

I looked up. "Children, how did Graham know that Knuffle Bunny was left behind?" I held up the book again. Soon children were pointing and whispering "It's right there."

"I hear what you're saying, children. Even though the words just say that Trixie and her Daddy leave the Laundromat, we know Knuffle Bunny has been left behind because we see it in the picture!"

I put the book down. "Looking at *Knuffle Bunny* made me realize that as you get your stories ready for publication, you might want to include extra information in your illustrations. That will give your reader important details."

❖ **Name the teaching point.**

"Children, today I want to teach you that you can study how authors use pictures to give their readers extra information. Then you can try to add details to your own illustrations to give your readers additional information too."

◆ COACHING

You might be asking, "What's the difference between a sketch and an illustration?" After all, your children have been sketching for months, if not years. We think of sketches as "sketching to write." It's a prewriting tool, to help your children pin down their stories, develop dialogue and inner thinking, capture details—all of which they'll then try to transfer to their text. Illustrations, though, are usually added after the story is written, and they highlight special moments, or add special details that aren't in the text. It's not worth it to color a sketch, or even finish it. An illustration, though, can enliven a story, or even tell part of it.

GRADE 1: FROM SCENES TO SERIES

TEACHING

Recall that writers study mentor texts to get ideas, and invite the children to investigate the pictures in your mentor text. Demonstrate by investigating one picture yourself, remarking on what you find out in the picture that wasn't in the text.

"Writers, remember that it's always good to study favorite mentor texts. Let's study a book we know is a favorite . . . *Henry and Mudge and the Happy Cat.*" I opened the book. "I'm going to ask myself—and you should also be thinking of this question—what happens in this picture, what extra details are there? The words say . . . 'One night Henry and Henry's father and Henry's big dog Mudge were watching TV.' But the picture tells us . . . " I let the children see the picture. They were soon pointing and murmuring.

"The picture shows that Henry and his father and Mudge were watching TV on a big gray couch, but the couch wasn't big enough for all of them, so Mudge ended up on their laps. And the room must have been warm and cozy, because Henry's dad has his shoes off."

I kept holding the book open to this page. "What have I learned here that I could try? Hmm . . . a picture can tell the reader extra details about the setting—where the characters are and what it looks like. In this case, I learned from the picture that the characters are all crowded onto a couch, in a warm and cozy place, all extra details about the setting!

"Hmmm. I'm thinking that I could add in some details into the setting of one of my stories about Sam. For example, in the story about Sam bringing home the wrong dog I could add an illustration that shows the other owner leashing her dog next to Sam's dog. That way, the reader knows that Sam might have a big decision to make even before Sam does!"

ACTIVE ENGAGEMENT

Invite your students to do the same work. Turn to some pages in your mentor text that have detailed illustrations so they can investigate the pictures.

"Writers, I'm going to read you some pages, and show you some of the pictures, from our mentor text. As I read, I'll pause, so you and your partner can really investigate what details you find out from the pictures. As we go to each page, if you notice an important detail, give a thumbs up so you can share some of what you find with your partner."

I opened the story to the next page and read, "Suddenly Mudge ran to the door and barked." I paused and read the print on the opposite page. "Henry's father opened the door. Sitting on the steps was the shabbiest cat Henry had ever seen." The children put thumbs up, and began to talk. I listened in, so I'd know who to call on.

You can decide how specifically you will refer to "author" versus "illustrator." Some writers illustrate their own picture books. Others don't. If you were going to be super authentic, you would study an author such as Tomie DePaola, who illustrates his own books—as your children do. We decided not to get into that discussion here for efficiency's sake, but it could be a rich conversation.

At first, you may feel as if the pictures don't give much added detail. That's partly, though, because you've synthesized the details in the pictures into your understanding of the story. Look again! Tell your kids, "Look again!"

Restate what children say, so that it is generalizable for what writers might do to convey information to their readers.

Mohammad said, "We noticed that even though Mudge is barking, his tail is wagging."

I expanded on what Mohammad said. "Yes, it's true, the words say Mudge barked, but the picture shows Mudge's tail is wagging. So that's like a secret clue for the reader that someone good is at the door."

Nora said, "It says Henry's father opened the door, but the picture shows Henry's father, Henry, and Mudge." She added, "And Mudge's tail is wagging there too."

I said, "Good noticing, Mudge's tail is still wagging there. That's one of those tiny, realistic details, isn't it?"

I motioned for the children's attention so we could keep going. Then I turned to the next page and read the description of the shabby cat. The children studied the picture intently. Before I was done, thumbs went up and they were whispering.

Miles offered, "The picture shows the cat has broken whiskers. It doesn't say that."

Robert added, "And the words make him sound ugly, but the pictures show that he's kind of cute. Ugly but cute. And he looks like he wants a home."

I put the book down and called the children's attention.

Debrief, again restating so the strategies are generalizable. Document the children's investigation on a chart. Then think aloud about your own story and what kind of details might be best in a picture.

"Writers, eyes on me. I think we've learned some important tips from our mentor text. We learned that writers sometimes use pictures to give clues about the setting, to bring characters to life, to tell secrets to the reader, and to add extra realistic details." I put up one, two, three, and four fingers as I said this, and added these to the "Our Favorite Series Authors . . . " chart from Session 9, under the bullet "Add details to their pictures."

"Wow, writers! Who knew that pictures are so important to the story? It's like the writer is telling the reader all these extra details and secrets." I looked at the chart as if studying it and thinking hard. "I'm already thinking about how I can put the pink and black collars in the pictures in my story, so the reader will know before Sam does that he's got the wrong dog!"

Our Favorite Series Authors . . .

- Describe the setting (the place, the weather, the season, the time of day)
- Make the action exciting!
- Give a lot of details for new characters
- Add details to their pictures
  - Give clues about the setting
  - Bring characters to life
  - Tell their reader secrets
  - Add extra realistic details
- Make a pattern ("he worried about . . . he worried that . . . mostly he worried . . .")
- Add POP-OUT words
- Show characters' strong feelings in pictures
- Repeat action in pictures and words

LINK

Help children remember their publication date and make writing plans to be ready.

"Writers, I know that a lot of you will be dying to work on illustrations for your stories. It's important that you keep in mind our publication date—it's in just a few days! So a lot of you might find that you need to finish a story, or revise a story, before tackling the illustrations.

"Writers also make extra time for themselves. Some of you might also want to take your stories home, to add even more illustrations.

"So now, before you set out to work, why don't you look over your folder, reread what you were just working on, and make a plan as a writer. When you have a really smart plan, talk it over with your partner. Partners, writers help each other meet their publication deadlines. Give some smart advice here!"

By reminding students they have a publication date coming up, you are energizing them for the work they will do in these last few sessions of the unit, as they fix up their writing so that it is ready for readers. By offering choice, you are fostering independence while also tucking in reminders that before they spend the entire writing time illustrating their stories, they need to check to see if they have stories that need to be finished or revised.

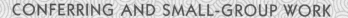

Using Questions to Prompt Students in Adding Details to Their Pictures

TODAY YOU MAY WANT TO GATHER A GROUP OF CHILDREN to give some guidance on adding detail to their pictures that will help them develop skills that you hope will eventually play out in their written texts. Here are some possibilities.

For writers whose stories seem to be missing important scenes or parts, you might gather this group of students and say, "Writers, I pulled you together because when I looked at your writing it seemed like parts may be missing. Like I wasn't quite sure where your character was. Or I couldn't really tell how he or she was feeling. Or what he or she was doing. That can happen to any writer. When you are writing fast and furious, sometimes you skip a part of the story. So I thought you could clear some of this up in your pictures."

You can then tell students that when writers add to their pictures, they imagine what all of the characters are doing and what all the things around them are doing. You might say, "One way writers do this imagining is they ask themselves questions, like, 'How does her body look? What will her face look like? What will people around the main character look like? What details can I add to the setting to show where the characters are and what is happening to them?'"

Another possibility is to gather some of your writers who often have creative ideas that they struggle to document in their written text, and remind them of how sometimes illustrations tell secrets to the reader. Show them the pages of *Good Night Moon*, for example, and all the secrets that are not in the words. Then, you might invite them to do this work as well, so that they can teach other writers. Miles, for instance, ran with this idea. He began to add thought bubbles to an illustration—and in each thought bubble he showed the characters thinking different things in the same moment (see Figure 17–1). Even though Miles didn't write lots and lots of words yet, in terms of his thinking, Miles was doing the Common Core reading work of grade five, which is to think about the different perspectives characters have in the same moment! With a little encouragement, Miles finished his illustration so that I could highlight it as a midworkshop teaching tool.

MID-WORKSHOP TEACHING Using Pictures to Show What Characters Are Thinking About

"Writers, eyes on me. I want to share what some of your friends have added to their pictures to give their reader more details.

"Miles has this story about his character, Max. On the first page of the story Max wakes up and runs downstairs to ask his mom if he can go to the park. He already had a picture of Max going downstairs, and his words described Max's action. Today Miles added some thought bubbles in a few places to give the reader more details that are not in the words."

I held up the first page to show the picture for all the kids to see (see Figure 17–1), and read aloud as well.

"Look, he added Max thinking about the playground. Now we can see that Max really wants to go to the park. Then . . . get ready. This part is funny. The dog and cat are thinking too!" A burst of laughter filled the room. "The dog is thinking about a bone and the cat is thinking about a mouse! Now we not only know what Max loves but also what his dog and cat love too! Miles did a great job adding some details to really keep the reader engaged.

"Thumbs up if you can imagine showing what different characters are thinking in one of your stories!"

Thumbs went up.

"Great. Let's get back to work."

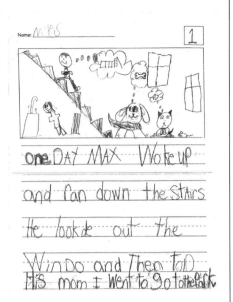

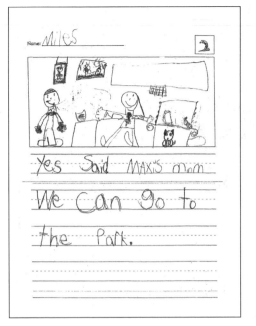

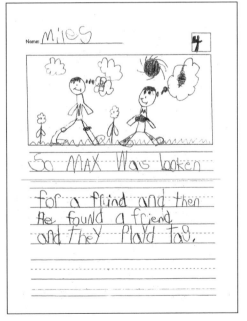

FIG. 17–1   Miles shows how his characters each think and feel differently in one moment of his story by using thought bubbles.

Digging Deeper with More Mentor Texts

Teach students that pictures can also show the reader *how* the character is feeling.

"Writers, I was so impressed by how you managed to use our mentor text as a teacher today. I noticed many of you continued to look closely at the illustrations to see how Cynthia Rylant included important details to help the reader and to tell the story.

"For example, Etta and Piper noticed that the picture on page 37 of *Henry and Mudge and the Happy Cat* shows that Henry is sad, even though the words don't say it. That's something I bet a lot of you can do in your pictures too—show how your character is feeling rather than telling it in words."

Set students up to investigate other mentor texts in the classroom, to notice what details are included in the pictures that they could try in their own fiction books.

"I was thinking there are other books we know and love that have pictures that help the reader in many ways. Let's take a few minutes and hunt around the library for books with illustrations that are important to the story. Check our read alouds, and your baggies, and favorites in the baskets."

After a few minutes, I invited kids to share what they found.

Amos and Jack found that in the book *Knuffle Bunny* the pictures show that the dad is upset, but the words don't say it.

Sophia and Nora noticed that in the book *Ella Sarah Gets Dressed* there is a two-page spread of pictures and no words at all. The reader can really see from the pictures that Ella is in her bedroom searching through her dresser drawers for clothes to wear.

"Let's steal some of these ideas, writers! If you want to take paper home so you can work on more pictures at home, do so. I am so glad you are taking all the parts of your stories so seriously. Great work, writers!"

"Meet the Author" Page

EXPERIENCED TEACHERS know that the more you get kids excited about the final product, the more they'll work at elaboration and revision. All this week, you've been playing up the serious role your kids are enacting as they prepare their series for publication.

Here, you'll hearken back to a few prior lessons. One is an early session from this unit of study, when you taught students to introduce their character in the first book of their series. Another occurred way back when you first introduced information writing, in Unit 2, *Nonfiction Chapter Books*. In that unit, you taught students that writers teach their readers important information, and they organize this information into categories, or chapters, headings, and subheadings. And even earlier, in *Small Moments*, you invited students to tell true stories about their lives.

Now your first-graders have a chance to converge all that expertise to create an "about the author" page to accompany their series. This is where they can tell the reader about themselves, in the genre of an introduction to a famous author. If you are digitally adept, you might print out small photos of your students to include as head shots. Students might think about what they would want to hold if they are posing as an author. Some will want to hold a pen, others will want to pose in front of their first series, and others will want to dress up like their character. They might study the author photographs on the backs of books and on authors' websites.

As your children take up this work, encourage them to go on with it in their spare minutes. They might interview each other, or seek out blurbs from other famous authors for their own books. They might go back and add blurbs to their first series, and then write ones that start, "Since her first series, so and so has been. . . . " They might collect their information books, and small moments, and list those as "prior publications."

All of this hoopla helps children to take their own writing seriously and to create a sense of audience and authentic publication.

IN THIS SESSION, you'll teach students that writers introduce themselves to their readers with "meet the author" pages for their series.

GETTING READY

✔ Sample "meet the author" pages from various authors, especially Cynthia Rylant (see Connection)

✔ Your own author page to use in the teaching part of the lesson

✔ "Meet the Author" list, prewritten (see Teaching)

✔ Chart paper and markers (see Active Engagement)

✔ Post-its for the conferring

COMMON CORE STATE STANDARDS: W.1.3, W.1.5, RL.1.1, SL.1.1, L.1.1, L.1.2

"Meet the Author" Page

CONNECTION

Allude to the upcoming publishing celebration and get your kids excited to be famous authors.

"Well, writers, it has been impressive to see you getting your second series ready for publication. I can tell your second series will make you even more famous. They'll certainly be beautiful additions to our library now, and you'll spend a lot of time reading each other's stories, I know. I've saved space here, on top of these shelves, for your new boxed sets."

I gestured toward a clean, empty shelf awaiting their work.

"Writers, there is something you can add to your series that publishers often add when a writer is a more famous author, like you are now." The children looked intrigued.

"I'm talking, of course, about a 'meet the author' page. I'm sure you've seen some of these in books you've read." I pointed to some of the books I had open on the floor, which showed the "meet the author" picture and blurb.

❖ **Name the teaching point.**

"Writers, today I want to teach you that as writers get ready to publish, they often include a 'meet the author' page to introduce themselves, and their writing, to their reader. You might consider including a 'meet the author' page for your series as well."

Some teachers have made "coming soon" announcements to ready readers for upcoming publications. Placing these announcements on shelves and around the school builds excitement for publication—and makes it very authentic.

TEACHING

Introduce the "meet the author" page and explain what kind of information is often included.

"Let me explain what a 'meet the author' page is, writers, and then we can try making one together. A 'meet the author' page introduces the author to the reader. I researched these, and I found out that a 'meet the author' page might include some of this information." I gestured toward a list I had prepared and read aloud.

Etta

My name is Etta and I live in Brooklin. I like to Play Sockr. I rite poems about my family. I have a brudr and sistr. I play the youkalaylee and I wont rite about it.

FIG. 18–1 Etta's "meet the author" page

"Meet the Author" Tells About

✓ Favorite hobbies
✓ Our family
✓ Our pets
✓ Where we live
✓ Where we get our ideas
✓ What we've written before
✓ What we'll write next

Demonstrate what your "meet the author" page might sound like. Show how you turn to the chart to help you create one, and play up the "famous author and series" work you've all done.

"So my meet the author page might introduce me by telling about what I love and about my stories . . . Let's see." I turned and studied the chart and then said, slowly, "She loves children and she loves animals, especially dogs. That's why so many of her stories have children and dogs in them. She doesn't know any boys named Sam, but the character is based on her nephew, Graham, who loves dogs, even if he is a little afraid of them. Her first series was the famous Gretchen series, about a girl who builds a secret tree fort in the woods. Dog Trouble is her second series. This summer, she'll be hard at work on her third series, which readers predict will be about cats!

"That gives a lot of information about me, right? I should jot some of that down before I forget, though I guess I can use this list to remind me if I forget what I wanted to write."

ACTIVE ENGAGEMENT

Invite the children to make a "meet the author" page for your shared class series.

"Okay, let's try this together. Let's make a 'meet the author' page for the series we wrote together, the series about Joe and his bikes. Let's call the series Riding with Joe! and let's make our 'meet the author' page about us—Class 101." The kids nodded. I gestured toward the "meet the author" chart.

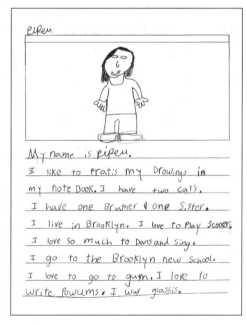

piper

My name is piper. I like to pratis my Drowings in my note Book. I have two cat's. I have one Bruther & one sister. I live in Brooklyn. I love to Play scooer, I love so much to Dans and sing. I go to the Brooklyn new school. I love to go to gym. I love to write powums. I war glassis.

FIG. 18–2 Piper's "meet the author" page

"Go ahead. Give this a try. Why don't you and your partner each come up with a few things we should include in our 'meet the author' page for Class 101? We have a lot of authors, so we can include a lot of information! What are some of the most important things we should tell our readers?"

I listened in as the children invented, and I jotted notes when they came up with details about the whole class. Then I called their attention back.

Share back what the kids have invented, showing them what a "meet the author" page might look like and sound like.

"Writers, eyes on me. I love hearing all the details you want to tell our readers. Let me say back some of what you said might go on our 'meet the author' page. Let's see, it might sound like . . . " I jotted just the first few lines on a piece of chart paper, so the kids would have a model later.

> Meet Class 101, the authors of the exciting series, Riding with Joe! Class 101 lives in New York City. Don't miss their famous first series, Charlie Rides Around. Class 101 . . .

"Okay, we can add to this later. It's great the way you told the reader so much important information—and made the reader want to read the series! Maybe we can take some pictures of us as authors too. We'll really make our readers eager to read these famous series!" I drew a box where our class picture could go on our "meet the author" page.

LINK

Review how children might use their time as writers. Remind them that publishing is just a couple of days away, and they can help each other make smart choices and get ready to publish.

"Writers, let's just review for a moment your choices for how you might use your time today. You might be revising and editing your stories. You might be working on your boxed sets or your illustrations. You might be adding 'meet the author' pages. Our publishing party is set for two days from now, so by the end of today, you might want to check in with your partner and talk about what work you still have left to do. Writers try to make smart choices about how to use their time. And writers help each other!"

Your language will excite the children. Using words such as famous, notable, *and* thrilling *to refer to the series that's underway stirs up the glamour and suspense about their work coming to fruition.*

Goal Setting and Reflection

AT THIS POINT YOU ARE VERY CLOSE TO THE FINAL CELEBRATION, so you will want to get a real sense of who needs a push to be ready and who actually looks done. After you have assessed the situation you can prioritize the next steps for your class.

Over the last few days your students have worked on punctuation and adding details to illustrations, and now they have begun an author page. Your conferring and small-group sessions today may include goal-setting and reflection.

As students prepare for the celebration there will no doubt be things you taught that they may be forgetting in their series books. To assist students to set goals, you may decide to gather a group of kids in the meeting area with their partners. Three sets of partners works nicely. Ask them to bring one of their stories that they plan to celebrate, and have a handful of Post-its for each child. You might say something like, "Writers, I was noticing that you all have selected a fiction book that you think you can add more to. Well, since we are getting close to the finish line, I thought I could offer you a suggestion to help out. Take a look around at all our wonderful charts. As you know, these are all the things you have been learning to help make your writing stronger. I was thinking you and your partner could take a close look at the charts and place a Post-it with your name on it next to the things you plan to do in your writing so you are ready to celebrate! Sometimes making your plan public helps you to finish because you can get help from each other."

Send kids off for a minute and coach them as they place Post-its on strategies listed on the charts. Gather them back so they can announce their plans and then send them off to get to work!

Another option is to do the same activity, only instead of placing Post-its next to strategies they *plan* to do, they can place them next to items they have already done. Then, after you call students back, they can reflect on the goals they have achieved, giving them confidence to move forward with new goals and more revision ideas for their final pieces.

MID-WORKSHOP TEACHING   Writing Series Titles

"Writers, let me remind you of something you learned in other units we have done. Writers look back through their book and think, 'Which title will help my reader understand what my whole book is about? What's the really important part?' Then they come up with a title—just a few words—and a picture and check to make sure each page goes with that title.

"Thumbs up if you remembered that!

"Okay, so now you can get really fancy with titles and give your whole series a title that captures your character and your stories. Like Dog Trouble.

"You may decide to mention this big series title in your 'meet the author' page. And you might also want to check that all the titles of your stories in the series go with that series title."

Planning for Publication

Rally students for the upcoming publication and channel them to make a plan for their writing time so that their series books will be ready. Emphasize that writers are independent and use their time wisely.

"Writers, for today's share session you can stay at your writing spots because you will need some space to look through your folders. Okay, so pens down, please, and eyes on me."

I waited for their attention.

"Our celebration is only two days away! I am so excited! So I was thinking today you might want to make a plan for what you need to get done so your series is ready to celebrate. You can talk with your partners as you do this. First, I suggest you reread your fiction books and choose the ones you plan to share at the celebration. Then talk with your partner about some things you will do tomorrow so you can get right to work. Do you still have to finish a story? Will you edit and revise? Will you make a cover? Do you need to finish a 'meet the author' page? Remember, independent writers make a plan so that they can use their time wisely."

Getting Ready for the Final Celebration

ear Teachers,

During yesterday's share session, most likely your students made a plan to get ready for the celebration. We imagine today will look like a busy workshop where kids get right to work allowing plenty of time to revise, edit, and make their work beautiful and ready to celebrate. Today you can remind them to make smart choices, turn to partners if they need help, and reference the charts in the room to help keep them going.

MINILESSON

In your connection you might want to refer to the list below. You could hang this chart of possible jobs the kids can do and coach them to choose from the list. Most kids will probably do all the things on the list.

Are You Ready to Celebrate?

✓ Finish any stories
✓ Work on covers, chapters for stories
✓ Work on editing: spelling, capitalization, quotations
✓ Add punctuation
✓ Add pictures
✓ Make boxed sets
✓ Work on "meet the author" page

During the teaching and active engagement you may invite kids to say out loud their plans for the day so they feel committed. Kids will most likely work closely with their partners as they reference the list and get busy working, so they can meet with each other during the minilesson prior to getting started. Even though they may have made plans yesterday, it will be a good reminder, and partners can hold each other accountable.

COMMON CORE STATE STANDARDS: W.1.3, W.1.5, W.2.3, RFS.1.4, SL.1.1, SL.1.6, L.1.1, L.1.2

After partners have had a chance to go over their plans, send students off to work like the wind at their To-Do list. While it may seem like a lot of work, if students are focused, they can easily accomplish everything they planned for.

CONFERRING AND SMALL-GROUP WORK

We imagine your small-group and conferring work will be led by the students. Allow them to lead your focus. After all, they have set forth a plan to be ready for the celebration. You might want to ask, "What are your plans? Can you show me what you have been doing? What are you planning to do next?" Then you can help them get ready or redirect their efforts if they seem off course. You may notice kids without a plan and will want to help them make one. If you notice kids are finished and look like they have nothing left to do, you can have them revise other pieces in their folders even if they do not plan on celebrating them, or for fun they can start writing a new book. The important thing is that you don't have a workshop in which kids are sitting around not working. On a day like today it will be unlikely since they have a lot of options to choose from and can always have fun creating and decorating their boxed sets. It is good to be ready and on the lookout for those kids just in case, though.

MID-WORKSHOP TEACHING

For your mid-workshop teaching it is important to keep the pace going so that everyone will be ready to celebrate. So you can either do the silent cheer shout-outs again (from Session 15) or remind the kids to check in with partners, or perhaps you'll notice something one of your students has done that you think is worthwhile to share with the class. Sharing what one student is doing to finish her series by the end of workshop time may help motivate other students to work hard to finish as well. You might also notice something on the chart that could use attention.

SHARE

At the end of the workshop during the share, you can prepare children for the celebration tomorrow. You may decide to go over the logistics. You can also pull the kids together and have them practice reading their pieces aloud to their partners so they are ready to share with an audience.

Good luck!

Christine and Mary

A Celebration of Series Writers
The Grand Finale!

ear Teachers,

Today you have a lot to celebrate! We hope this letter offers some inspiration for what you can do to end this unit. We encourage you to have fun and be creative as you celebrate not only your students' writing and the learning that took place, but also your great teaching! You did it! You managed to turn first-graders into serious series writers.

Along the way you may have "saddled up" for a revision party or even turned editing time into a punctuation party, too. However, this is the *grand finale!* This is the time to showcase *all* the writing skills, creativity, and hard work that happened in this unit of study to an audience who will admire the work.

Keep in mind that a celebration is an opportunity for reflection, thinking about next steps, and time for some *fun*.

By today kids will already have decided on a book or perhaps a boxed set that includes three fiction books that they want to share at the celebration. They also will have revised, edited, and fancied up their writing.

So, today is the day to honor it all. Below are some suggestions for ways to honor your students and their writing.

CELEBRATION

You may decide to invite kindergarten students to come in for a class visit to mingle around the room to meet the first-grade authors. After all, they will be first-graders soon, and it could be a fun way to get them excited to move up to first grade.

You can also invite the second-grade teachers. The kids can show off all that they already know about writing to their teachers for next year.

If you have not had parents in yet for a writing celebration, this is a great opportunity to do so.

COMMON CORE STATE STANDARDS: W.1.3, W.2.3, RFS.1.4, SL.1.1, SL.1.6, L.1.1, L.1.2

Or you may decide to have another first-grade class who has also done the unit partner up together with kids in your class so they can swap stories and compare what they did.

You may be concerned about the logistics of a "meet the author" mingle-style celebration. One possibility is that it takes place in the school library. The kids can sit at various places spread out around the room with boxed sets in hand. As visitors enter the library they simply approach a student to hear a little bit about him or her and the series he or she wrote. In essence, the kids will introduce themselves as well as their characters. They can choose a section to read or maybe they will just flip through the pictures. Or they can allow the visitors to read on their own.

Cynthia Rylant has written a biography titled *Best Wishes*. In it, she writes about her interests, her family, her home, and how these things are what keep her writing. These are inspirations for her books. We are not suggesting kids write a biography, although they will have a "meet the author" page. We are suggesting that perhaps reading this book to your kids will give them a sense of what they can say to people who want to meet them and see their books.

AFTER THE CELEBRATION

We imagine you will want to make this momentous occasion grand. Perhaps the celebration will end with the kids placing their books on the *school* library shelves. This feels bigger than the classroom library, which they have probably already done many times. Ahead of time, you can arrange with the librarian to clear some shelves and designate some space for the new books.

As a way to ground all of this so that the incredible learning continues, you may decide to have the kids name three big things they learned as a writer. You can chart this and display it at the celebration in the library.

In addition, you might ask the kids to make a plan for their next series, and they can design a few "Coming Soon" posters to hang in the library too. These may be books they write at home or over the summer. The message here is that they don't have to stop because the unit is over.

Whatever you decide to do to end this unit, we wish you well. Keep writing and have fun!

Christine and Mary

① Name: Annabel   Date:

One day Mary was going to a hug aqwaryum. Mary was on a feld chrep. She was on the bus. Mary was ixitid. Mary was fiding a set.

② Name: Date:

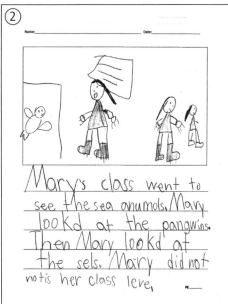

Mary's class went to see the sea anumols. Mary lookd at the pangwins. Then Mary lookd at the sels. Mary did not notis her class leve.

③ Name: Date:

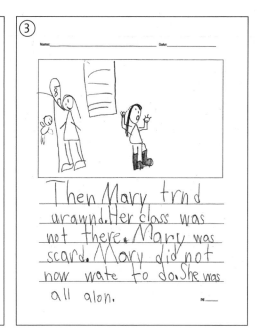

Then Mary trnd urawnd. Her class was not there. Mary was scard. Mary did not now wate to do. She was all alon.

④ Name: Date:

Mary lookd and lookd she coal not find her class. Mary fawnd sumone who wrkd there. "She said I am lost I can not find my class.enywar." The man said I will help you find your class littol girl. Mary was happy

⑤ Name: Date:

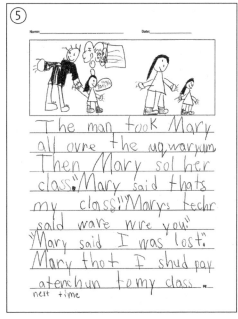

The man took Mary all ovre the aqwaryum. Then Mary sol her class. "Mary said thats my class!" Mary's techr said ware wre you!" "Mary said I was lost." Mary thot I shud pay atenchun to my class next time

FIG. 20–1   One of Annabel's fiction stories for her series

1

12/SM   Alejandra

Gilda's   pet
cat.

2

Name Alejandra   Date 12/7

One day Gilda was reading,
Gilda was bored, she decided
to play with her cat, Gilda's
cat was upside down
with her paws up, she was so
cute. Gilda's cat was
brown, white and black.

3

Name _____   Date _____

Moments later Gilda's cat
did not like the pedding
so Gilda's cat scrached
Gilda for no resort Gilda
yelled "mom! her mom came
qwkly   and   even   qwikly

4

Name _____   Date _____

Gilda's mom came and
said "what happend" Gilda said...
"the cat scrached me. Gilda
said to her cat... "bad
kitty". Gilda's mom said
"if you see a cat
                wagging its
            tail so
        much, don't
        touch it
        because it
        is mad

5

Name _____   Date _____

Gilda's mom put a
bandage on Gilda's hand.
Gilda felt much more
better. but before she put
the bandage on she washed
her hands and then she
            put on
            the purple
            mediom
            bandage.

FIG. 20–2   One of Alejandra's fiction stories for her series

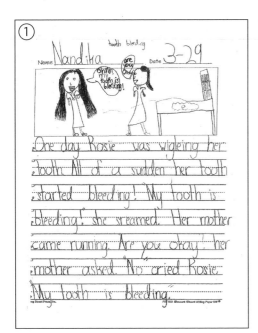

①

Name Nandika   tooth bleeding   Date 3-29

One day Rosie was wigleing her tooth. All of a sudden her tooth started bleeding! "My tooth is bleeding!" she screamed. Her mother came running. "Are you okay?" her mother asked. "No" cried Rosie. "My tooth is bleeding."

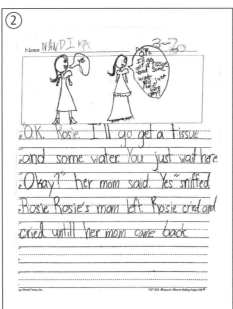

②

Name NANDIKA   Date 3-20

"OK. Rosie. I'll go get a tissue and some water. You just wait here. Okay?" her mom said. "Yes" sniffed Rosie. Rosie's mom left. Rosie cried and cried untill her mom came back.

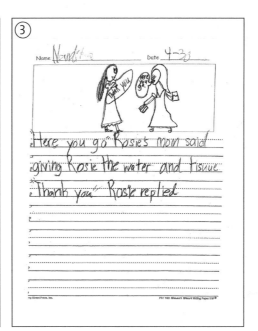

③

Name Nandika   Date 4-23

"Here you go" Rosie's mom said giving Rosie the water and tissue. "Thank you" Rosie replied.

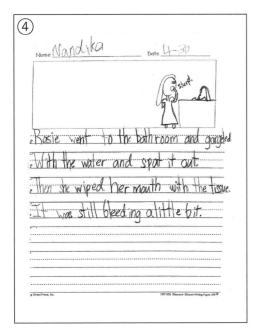

④

Name Nandika   Date 4-30

Rosie went to the bathroom and gargeled with the water and spat it out. Then she wiped her mouth with the tissue. It was still bleeding a little bit.

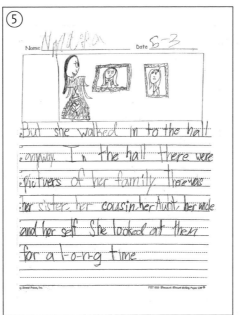

⑤

Name Nandika   Date 5-3

But she walked in to the hall anyway. In the hall there were pictures of her family. There was her sisters her cousin her aunt her uncle and her self. She looked at them for a l-o-n-g time.

FIG. 20–3   One of Nandika's final fiction stories for her series

1
Jenfre gos to the doctr.
by Syanna
2
Name: Syanna
Date: 1/3
My tummy hrts
I will brig you to the doctr
MOM Said "I will brig you to the doctr" and Jenfre Said ok. So they went to get thar cos and Skarf and mitins and they went osiend.
3
Name:
Date:
They both whent isied the tacsy.
pg 2
4
Name:
Date:
Obin
the doctr Said obin up Jenfre was nrvis and Skarn
pg 3
5
Name:
Date:
Jenffr
Mommy
doctr
Sorry
You trikt me
haha
MoM Said "You trikt me". Jenffr Said "Sorey" and the doktr Said "haaa!!!!!" and befor the doctr Said haaa She Said She is not sike
pg 4

FIG. 20–4 One of Syanna's final fiction stories for her series

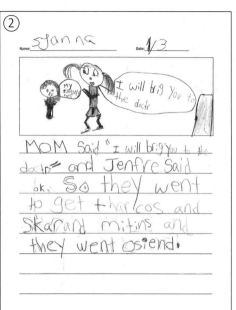

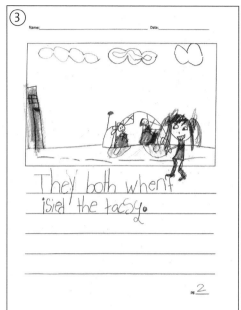

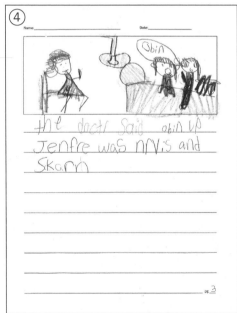

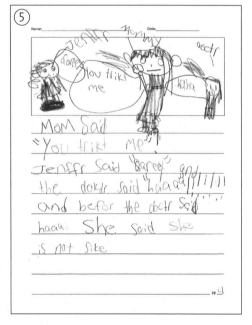

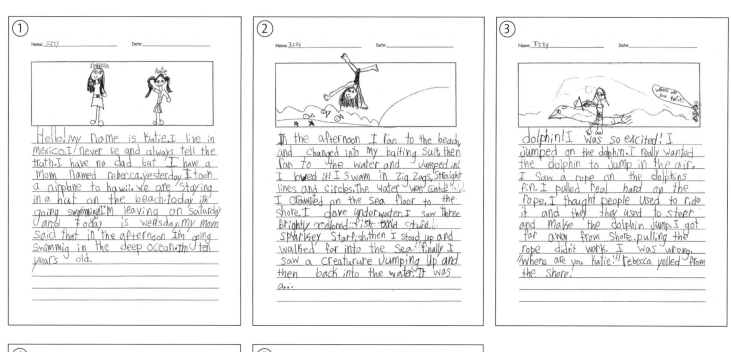

①

Name: Izzy   Date:

Hello! My Name is Katie. I live in Mexico. I never lie and always tell the truth. I have no dad but I have a Mom named rebecca. yesterday I took a airplane to hawii. We are staying in a hut on the beach. today im going swimming! I'm leaving on saturday and today is wensday. My mom said that in the afternoon I'm going swimmig in the deep ocean. Im ten years old.

②

Name: Izzy   Date:

In the afternoon I ran to the beach, and changed into my baiting suit, then ran to the water and jumped in! I loved it! I swam in Zig Zags, straight lines and circles. The water was cold! I crawled on the sea floor to the shore. I dove underwater. I saw three brightly colored fish and studied sparkey Starfish, then I stood up and walked far into the sea. Finally I saw a creaturure jumping up and then back into the water. It was a...

③

Name: Izzy   Date:

dolphin! I was so excited! I jumped on the dolphin. I really wanted the dolphin to jump in the air. I saw a rope on the dolphins fin. I pulled real hard on the rope. I thought people used to ride it and they they used to steer and make the dolphin jump. I got far away from shore. pulling the rope didn't work. I was wrong. "Where are you katie!" rebecca yelled from the shore.

④

Name: Date:

I looked back and saw Mom yelling for me. I pulled the rope again trieing to turn the dolphin to go toward Shore. But it still didn't work. I was afraid to jump of because I thought it was to deep and I could drown. I felt like I had to stay on the dolphin forever. I guessed maybe the dolphin can only hear dolphin langauge. Maybe I could comunicate to the dolphin and tell her to go to shore. but I didnt know dolphin launguage. "eek eek!" I yelled.

⑤

Name: Date:

Then I just realized I had a dolphin dictonary in my pocket. It tells how to speak dolphin language. I searched the book until I found the words I needed to say to the dolphin. "Eek week, eek!" I yelled. The dolphin stared at me. Then it turned toward shore. yay!! I yelled. "I did it!" I yelled again. when the dolphin got to shore I jumped on land and hugged rebecca. "thank you dolphin" I said. from then on katie never went anywere without her mom so she wouldn't get worrid.

FIG. 20–5   One of Izzy's final fiction stories for her series. Sometimes you'll see kids elaborating on their narratives by inserting fantasy elements; for example, riding on a dophin.

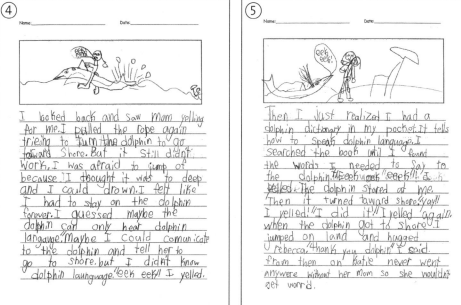